piano · vocal · guitar

contemporary gospel hits

2	Again I Say Rejoice	ISRAEL HOUGHTON
12	All Because of Jesus	ANDRAÉ CROUCH
19	All I Ever Really Wanted	DONNIE McCLURKIN
24	All That I Need	CECE WINANS
38	All Things Are Working	FRED HAMMOND
46	God Has Not 4Got	TONÉX
29	God Is Able	SMOKIE NORFUL
54	Hallelujah Praise	CECE WINANS
63	Heaven	MARY MARY
70	I Need an Angel	RUBEN STUDDARD
84	I Need You Now	SMOKIE NORFUL
92	I'll Trust You	RICHARD SMALLWOOD
96	Imagine Me	KIRK FRANKLIN
104	In Your Name	JOHN P. KEE
114	Look at Me Now	KIRK FRANKLIN
79	Mighty Wind	ANDRAÉ CROUCH
126	My Everything	RICHARD SMALLWOOD
144	Only You Are Holy	DONNIE McCLURKIN
135	Open My Heart	YOLANDA ADAMS
148	Shackles (Praise You)	MARY MARY
166	Shake Yourself Loose	VICKIE WINANS
178	Show Up!	JOHN P. KEE
157	The Storm Is Over Now	BISHOP T.D. JAKES
196	Turn It Around	ISRAEL HOUGHTON
188	Why Me	KIERRA "KIKI" SHEARD

ISBN 978-1-4234-3883-0

HAL•LEONARD®
CORPORATION
7777 W. BLUEMOUND RD. P.O. BOX 13819 MILWAUKEE, WI 53213

Visit Hal Leonard Online at
www.halleonard.com

AGAIN I SAY REJOICE

Words and Music by ISRAEL HOUGHTON
and AARON LINDSEY

With energy

Re- joice __ in the Lord __ al - ways, and a - gain __ I say, __ and a - gain __

__ I say __ re - joice __ in the Lord __ al - ways, __ and a - gain __

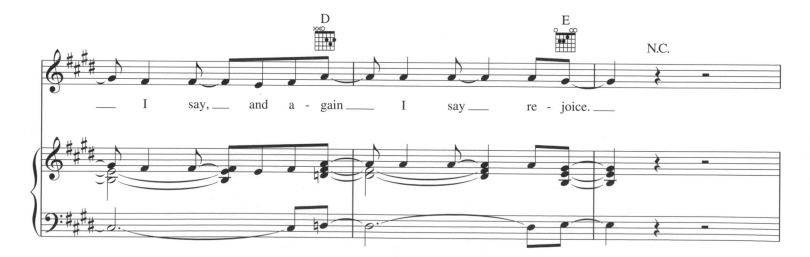

__ I say, __ and a - gain __ I say __ re - joice. __

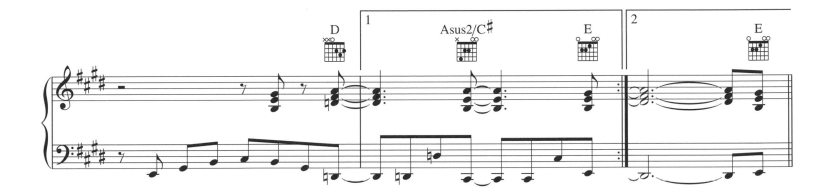

Come bless __ the Lord. Come bless __ the Lord. Draw near __ to wor-

-ship Christ, ___ the Lord and bless __ His name, His ho - ly name,

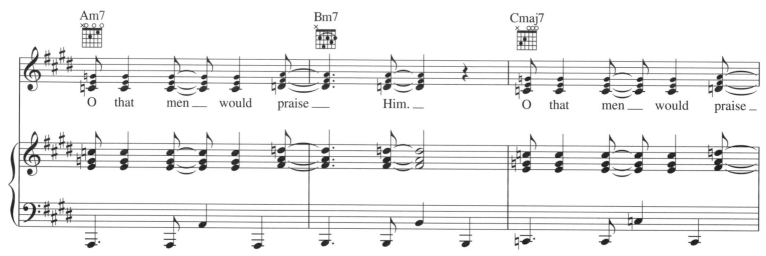

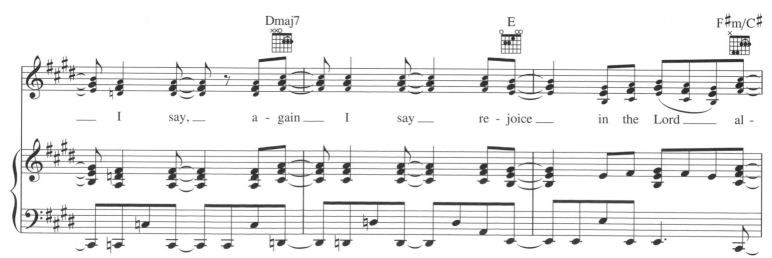

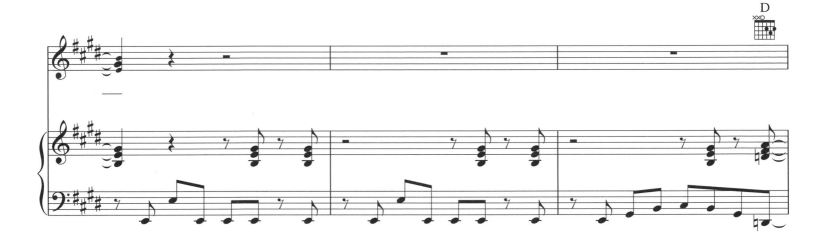

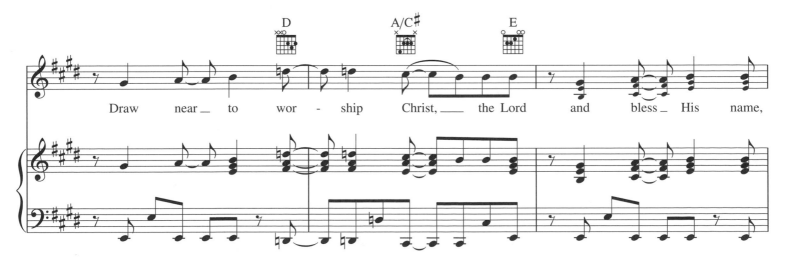

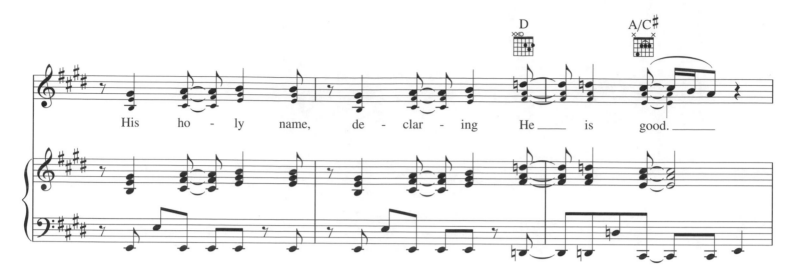

His ho-ly name, de-clar-ing He ___ is good. ___

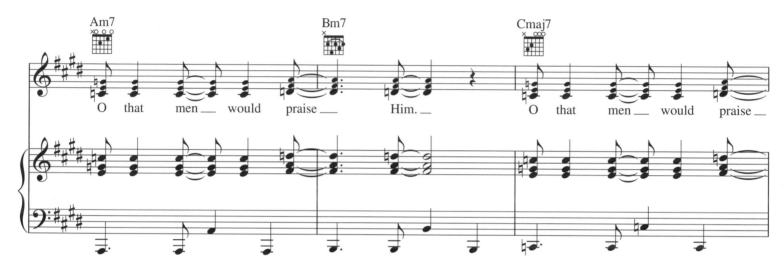

O that men ___ would praise ___ Him. ___ O that men ___ would praise ___

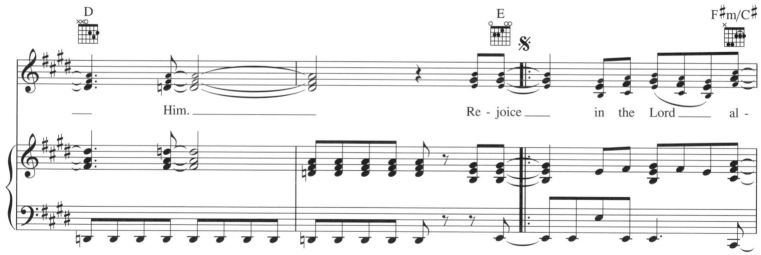

___ Him. _____ Re-joice ___ in the Lord ___ al-

- ways, ___ and a-gain ___ I say, ___ a-gain ___ I say ___ re-joice ___

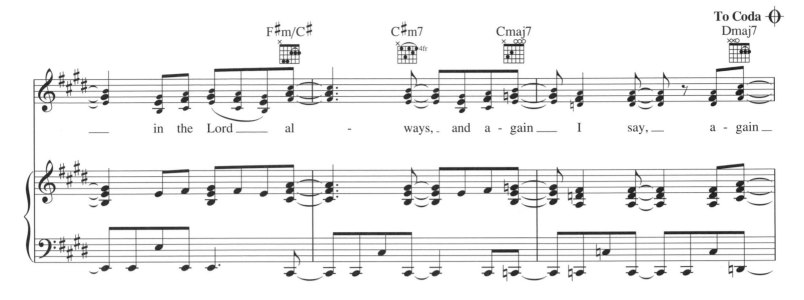

in the Lord ___ al - ways, ___ and a - gain ___ I say, ___ a - gain

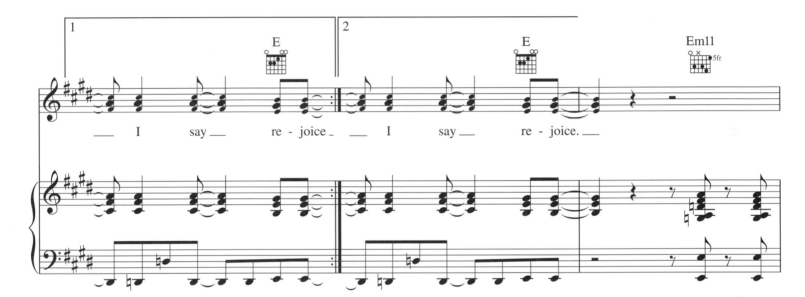

___ I say ___ re - joice ___ I say ___ re - joice. ___

__ in the Lord __ al - ways, __ and a - gain __ I say, __ a - gain __

__ I say __ re - joice __ in the Lord __ al - ways, __ and a - gain __

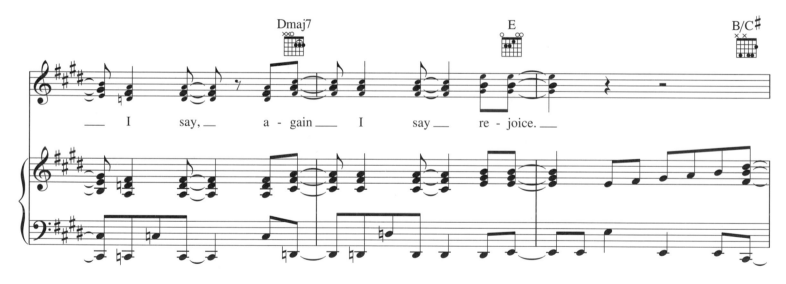

__ I say, __ a - gain __ I say __ re - joice. __

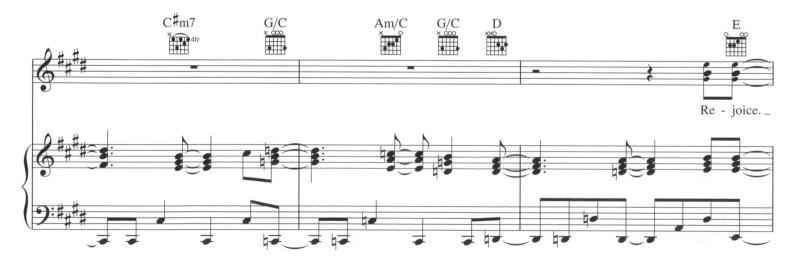

Re - joice. __

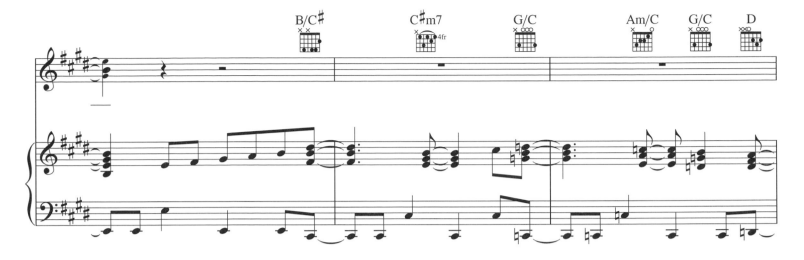

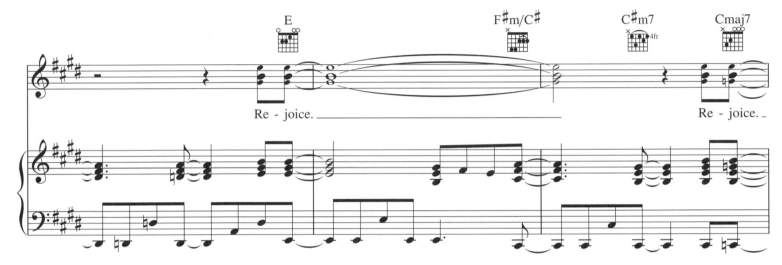

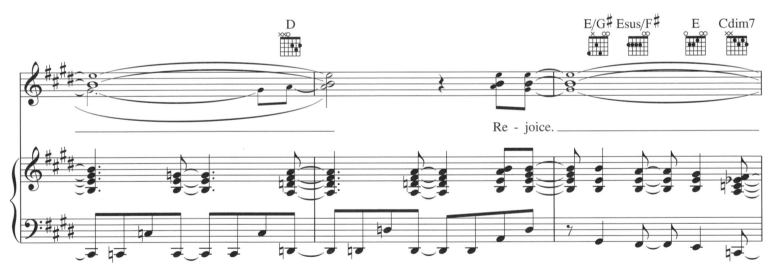

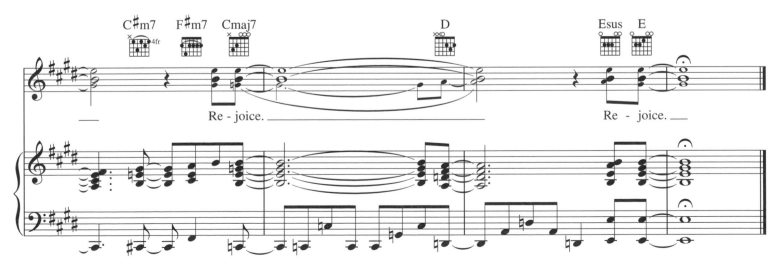

ALL BECAUSE OF JESUS

Words and Music by
ANDRAÉ CROUCH

Moderate Soul groove

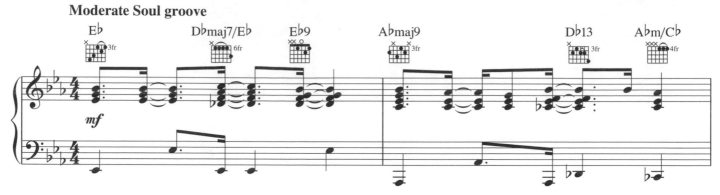

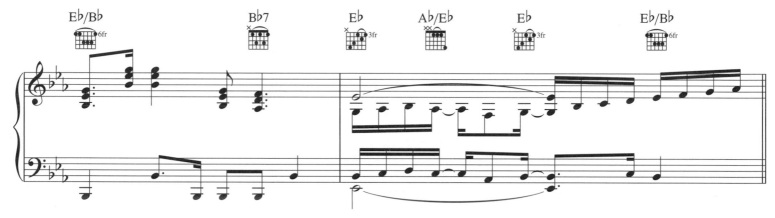

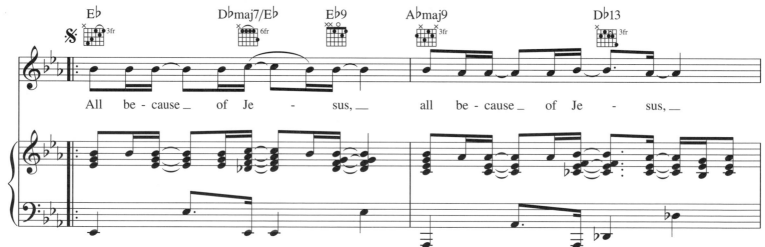

All be-cause_ of Je - sus,_ all be-cause_ of Je - sus,_

all be-cause_ of Je - sus we are here. Be-cause_

think that you should do __ the same. __ Since we __ are here, _____ to-

geth - er let's praise __ His name. __ Be - cause __ of Je - sus, _____ we ____ are

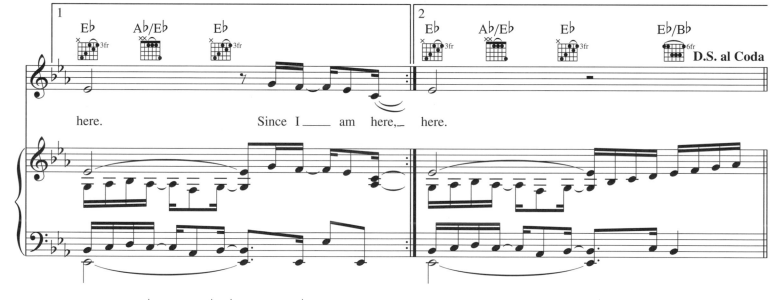

here.   Since I ____ am here, __ here.

here.   We have all   gath - ered   here, _

Oh, hal - le - lu - jah, we give Him the hon - or, give Him the praise. _

Oh, hal - le - lu - jah, we give Him the hon - or, give Him the praise. _

Play 4 times

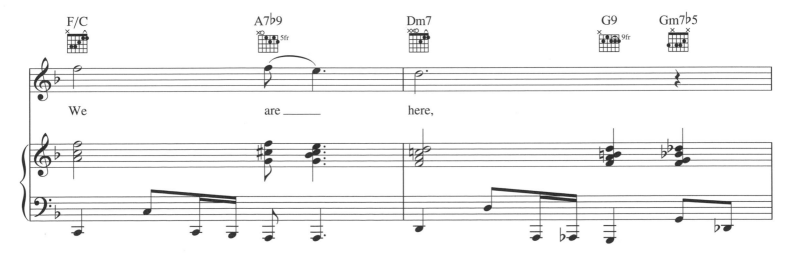

We are _____ here,

All I Ever Really Wanted

Words and Music by
DONALD McCLURKIN

Search-ing for a life-time for some things that sat-is-fy. _____ Paid a lot of pric-es, and so

man - y nights I've cried. _____ In my time of des - per - a - tion came a

sim - ple rev - el - a - tion, and that was, all I ev - er real - ly want - ed was _ You.

Thought I want-ed mon-ey and I thought I want-ed fame. _____
If there were a mor-al to the things that I have learned, ___

Thought it would ful-fill me, that's un - til it fi-n'ly came. _____ Then I
it would be to fol - low love, ev-'ry move and ev-'ry turn. _____ And the

sweet-ly heard _ You beck-on me, ___ yes, and it on-ly took _ one sec - ond to see,
time of sec - ond chanc - es, _____ what I found at sec - ond glanc - es is that

all I ev-er real-ly want-ed was _ You, yeah. ___ There were times I did-n't know

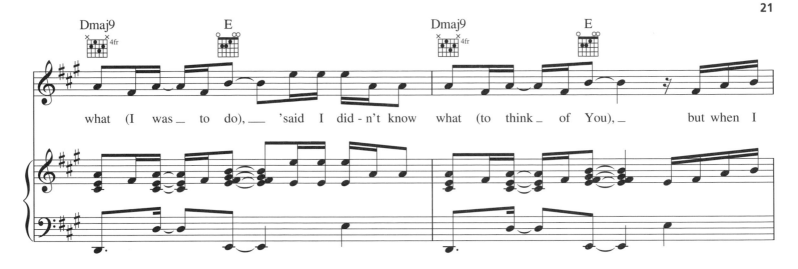

what (I was _ to do), _ 'said I did-n't know what (to think _ of You), _ but when I

turned a-round, _ I turned _ and found You were there all the time. _ I did-n't know

what (or where _ to go), _ I did-n't know what (I was _ to know), _ but You

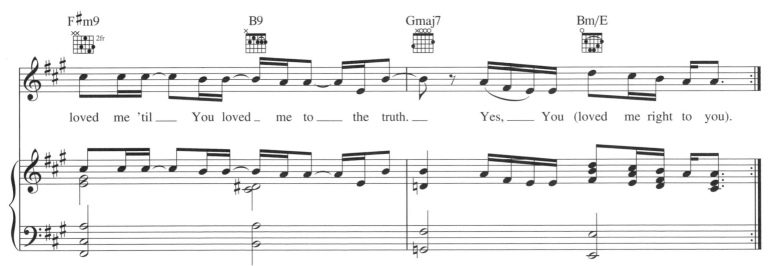

loved me 'til _ You loved _ me to _ the truth. _ Yes, _ You (loved me right to you).

If there were a mor-al for the things that I have learned, ___ it would be to fol-low love, ___ ev-'ry move and ev-'ry turn. ___ For in

time of sec-ond chanc-es, what I found at sec-ond glanc-es, is that

all I ev-er real-ly want-ed, You know, I've found in You. ___ Whoa, ___

all I ev-er real-ly want-ed, some-how I know it's true. __

(All I ev-er real-ly want-ed), You know I've found in __ You, yeah, __ yeah, yeah, yeah.

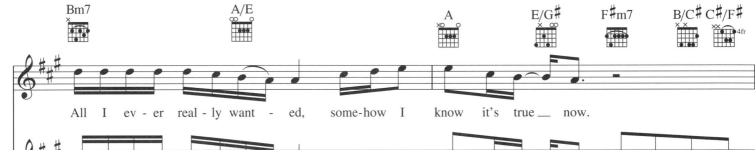

All I ev-er real-ly want-ed, some-how I know it's true __ now.

(All I ev-er real-ly want-ed) was __ You, _____ oh Lord. _____

ALL THAT I NEED

Words and Music by CECE WINANS
and KEITH THOMAS

Moderate Ballad

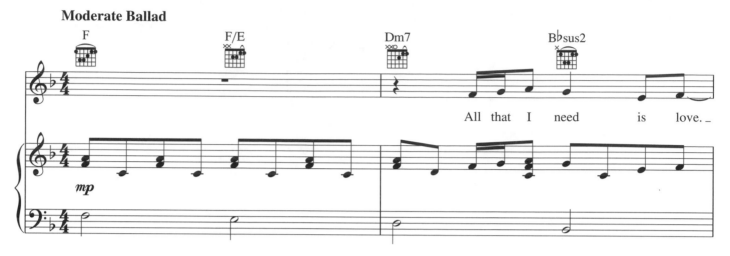

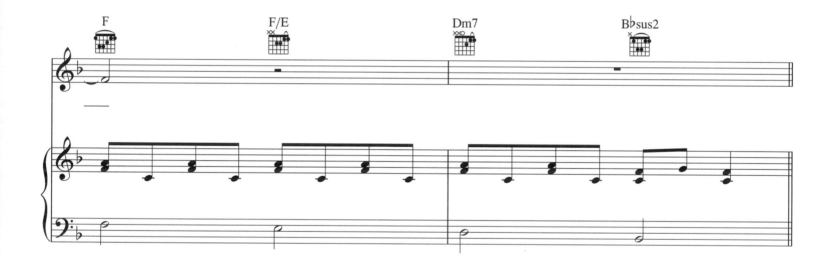

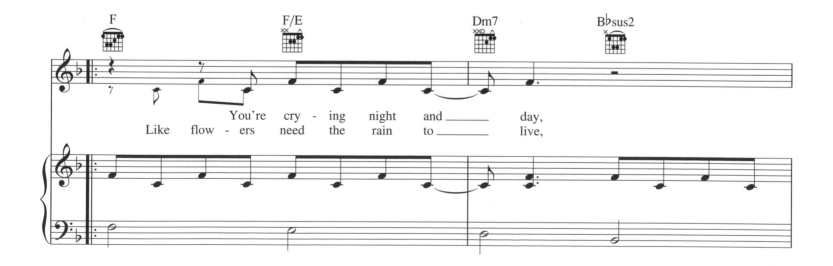

All that I need is love. _

You're cry - ing night and _____ day,
Like flow - ers need the rain to _____ live,

I you won-der how you ev - er lost your __ way.
de - pend __ on the great-est gift You __ give.

Noth - ing mat - ters, you must sur - vive. Your
You changed my mind for - ev - er,

heart is slow - ly dy - ing, and so you cry: }
lov - er of my life. __ I re - a - lize: }

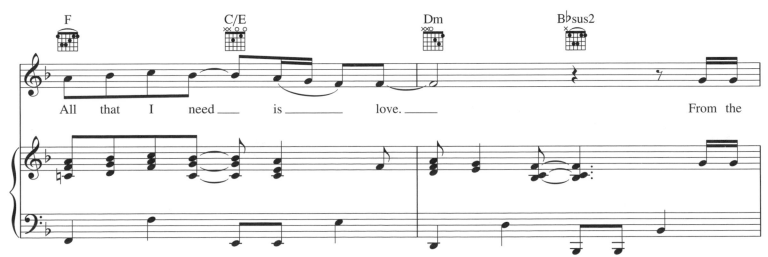

All that I need __ is __ love. __ From the

mo - ment I wake, ___ let me feel Your ___ em - brace.

All that I need ___ is _____ love. ____ Hold me

clos - er ___ each day, ev - 'ry step of ___ the way.

step of ___ the way. When the morn - ing comes _ and the

sun ____ ris - es to the sky, all my trou - bles will be o - ver and the

way made eas - y. Un - til then, all I need is to

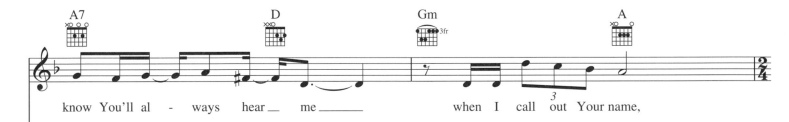

know You'll al - ways hear __ me ____ when I call out Your name,

call out Your name. ____

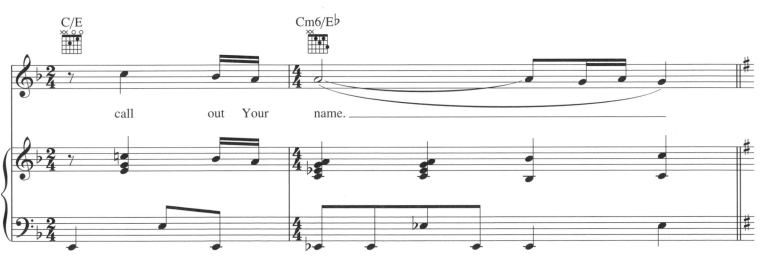

All that I need ___ is ___ love. ___ From the

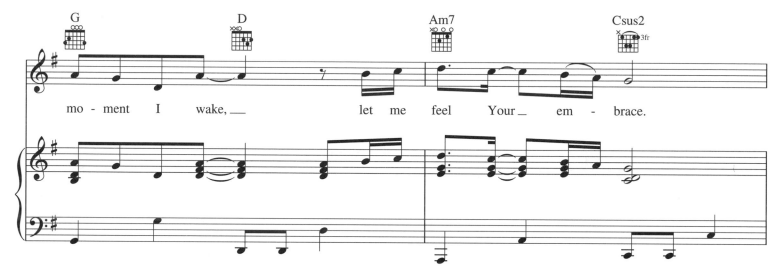

mo - ment I wake, ___ let me feel Your ___ em - brace.

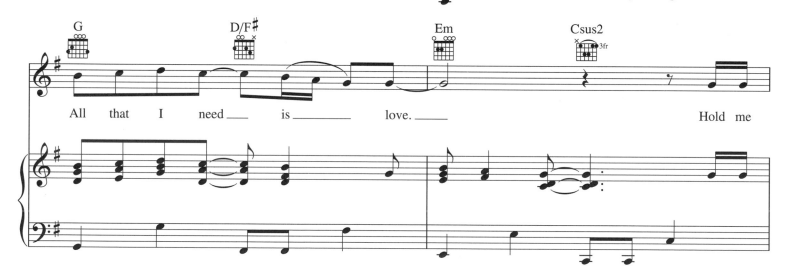

All that I need ___ is ___ love. ___ Hold me

Optional Ending

Repeat and Fade

clos - er ___ each day, ev - 'ry step of ___ the way.

GOD IS ABLE

Words and Music by
SMOKIE NORFUL

ALL THINGS ARE WORKING

Words and Music by FRED HAMMOND,
TOMMIE WALKER and KIM RUTHERFORD

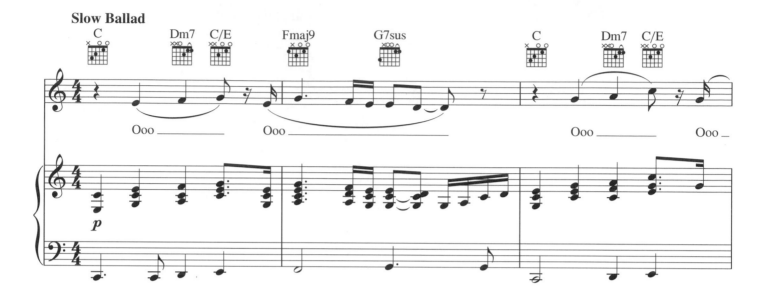

You say you'll re-treat. You say you just ___ can't win. ___

Be-fore you let your cir-cum-stance tell ___ you how ___ the sto-ry ends, know that His Word, ___

___ His Word says you can ___ stand. He'll cov-er you with His ___ grace. ___

Ev-'ry-thing you need is in your ___ hand, ___ so lift up your head ___ and say:

I'm in His hands and I'm on His __ mind. __ He prom-ised me He'd al-ways be __ there. __ By

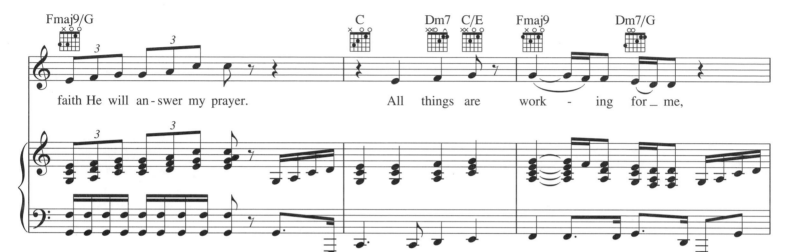

faith He will an-swer my prayer. All things are work-ing for __ me,

e - ven things I _____ can't see. __

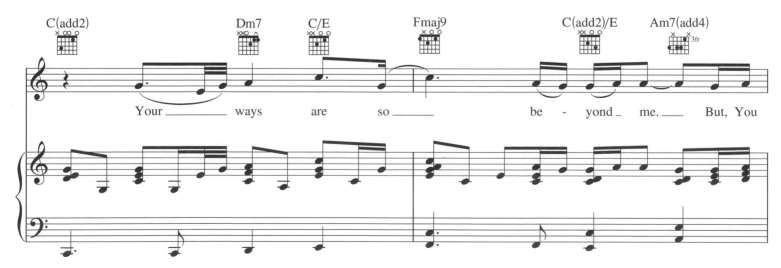

Your _____ ways are so _____ be-yond __ me. __ But, You

but say, "Lord, I love You more." And that is e-nough to know. _____ All things are

work - ing for _ me, e - ven things I _____ can't see. _

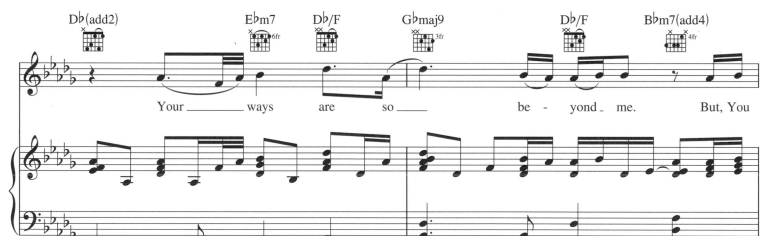

Your _____ ways are so _____ be - yond _ me. But, You

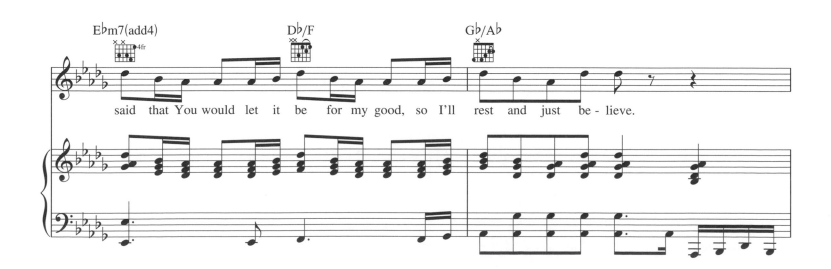

said that You would let it be for my good, so I'll rest and just be - lieve.

GOD HAS NOT 4GOT

Words and Music by
ANTHONY WILLIAMS II

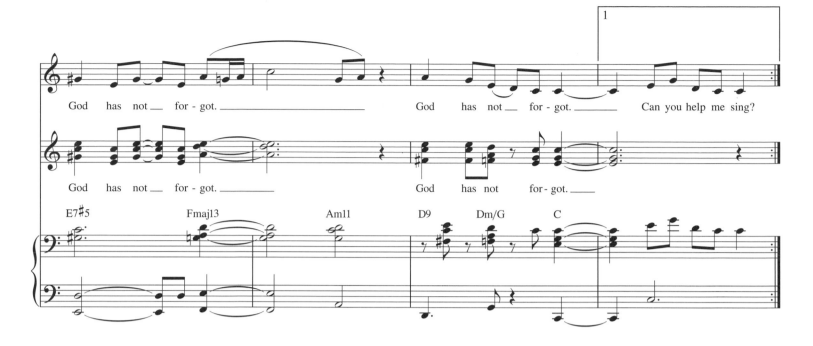

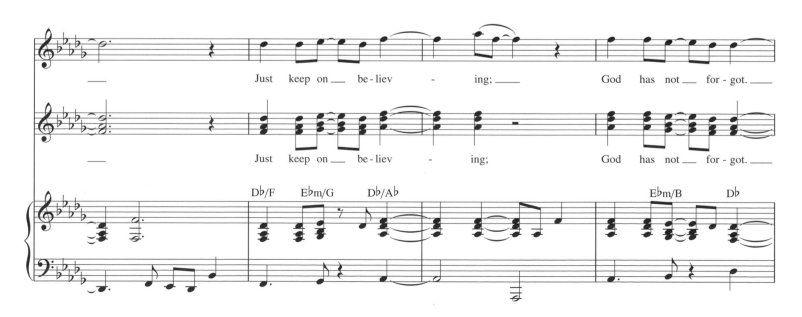

'Cause if He said that He would do it, it will come to pass.

If He said that He would do it, it will come to pass.

Bbm11 Eb7 Gb/Ab Bbm7

God has not for-got a-bout you, no. God has not for-got.

God has not for-got. God has not for-got.

F7#5 Gbmaj13 Bbm11 Eb9 G/Ab Db

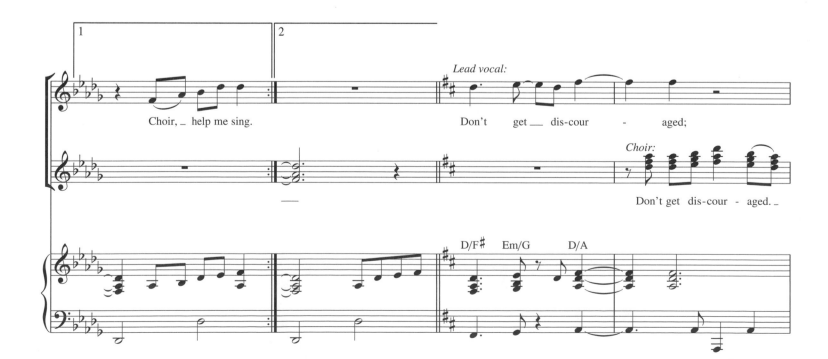

1 2

Lead vocal:

Choir, help me sing. Don't get dis-cour - aged;

Choir:

Don't get dis-cour - aged.

D/F# Em/G D/A

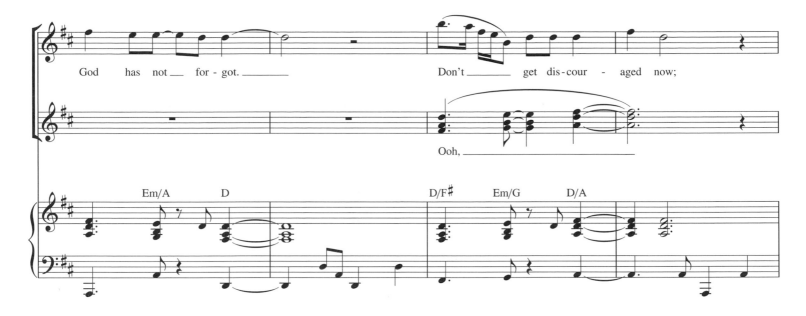

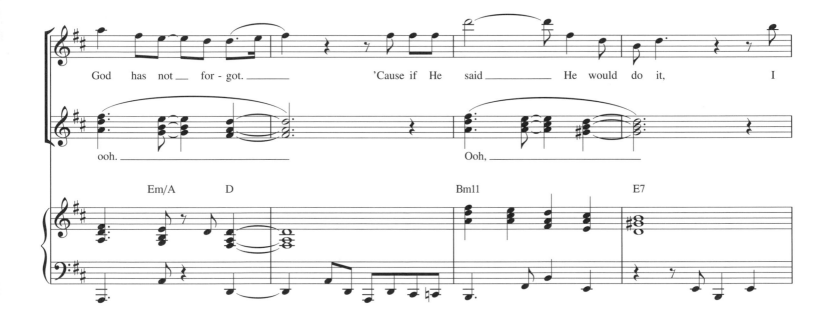

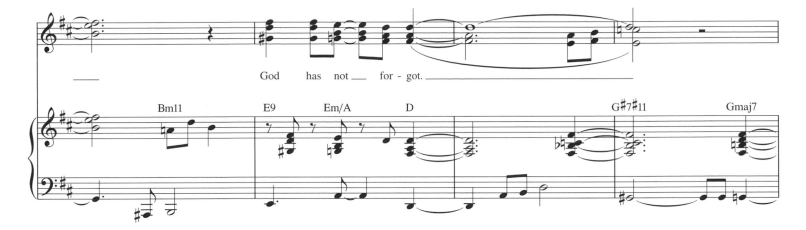

God has not __ for-got. __

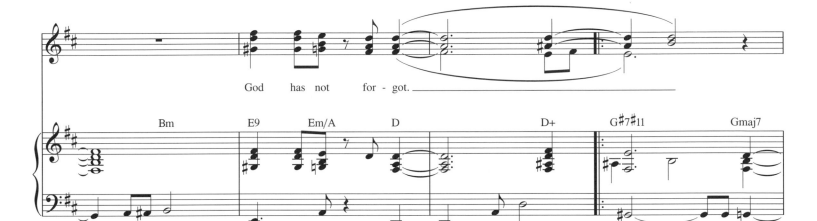

God has not for-got. __

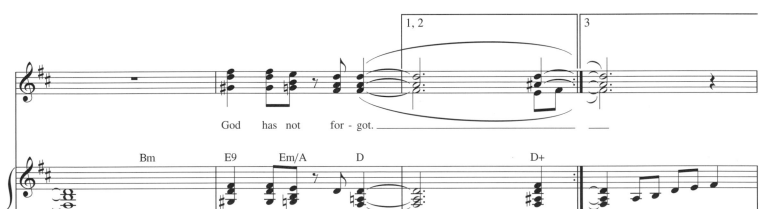

God has not __ for-got. __

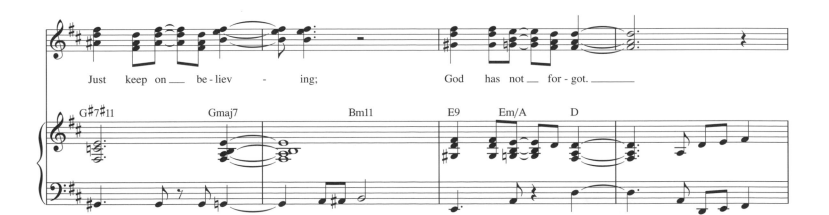

Just keep on __ be-liev - ing; God has not __ for-got.

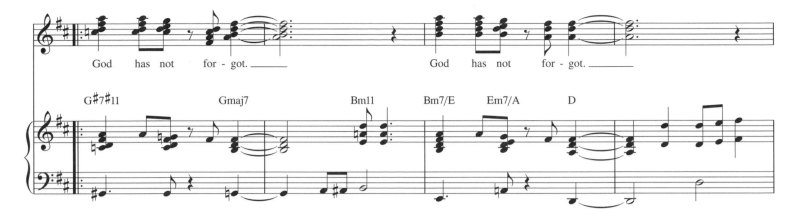

God has not for-got. _____ God has not for-got. _____

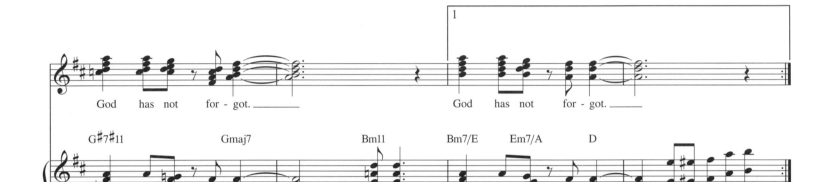

God has not for-got. _____ God has not for-got.

God has not for-got. _____

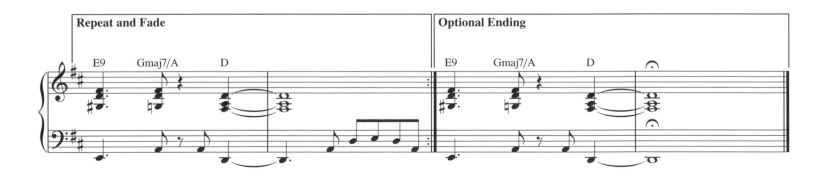

Repeat and Fade

Optional Ending

HALLELUJAH PRAISE

Words and Music by CECE WINANS,
CEDRIC CALDWELL and VICTOR CALDWELL

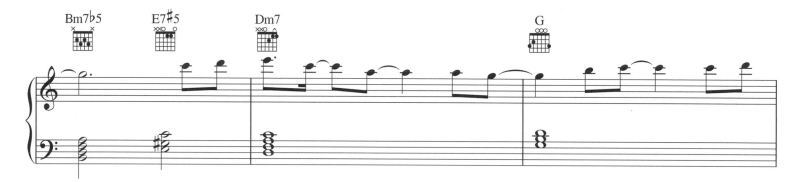

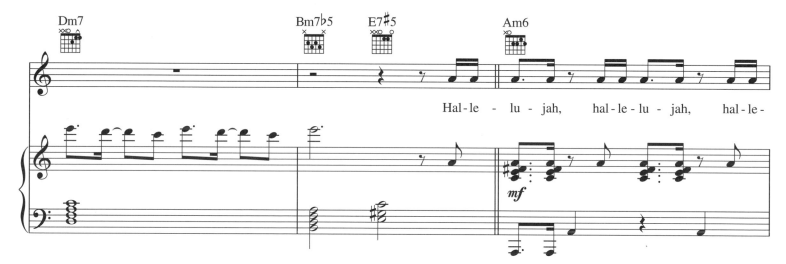

Hal-le - lu - jah, hal-le - lu - jah, hal-le -

lu - jah. Hal-le - lu - jah, hal-le-lu - jah, hal-le - lu - jah.

* Recorded a half step lower.

Hal - le - lu - jah is the high - est praise, _ hal - le - lu - jah is the high - est praise. _

Hal - le - lu - jah is the high - est praise, _ hal - le - lu - jah is the high - est praise. _

G/A   D13   G9

Let ev - 'ry - thing that hath breath _ praise the Lord. Come on and sing, be

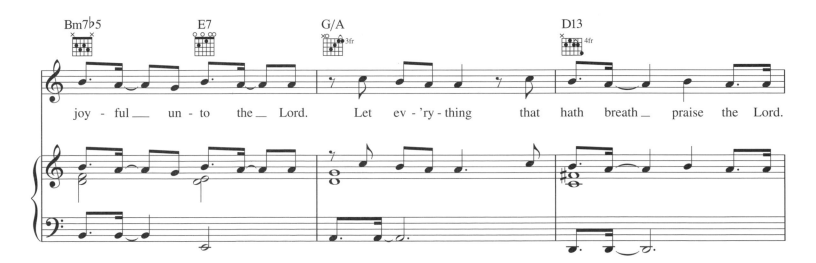

Bm7♭5   E7   G/A   D13

joy - ful _ un - to the _ Lord. Let ev - 'ry - thing that hath breath _ praise the Lord.

Come on and sing, let, let ev-'ry, let ev-'ry - thing. Sun and the moon, all
thing. Let the high praise be

stars of ___ light, He com-mand - ed ___ and they were ___ cre - at -
in your ___ mouth. Bless His ho - ly name for - ev -

- ed. Ooh, ooh, ooh, ooh. Oh, trum - pets sound through -
- er. Young and the old, all

out the ___ earth for the Lord is good ___ and great - ly to ___ be praised.
God's chil - dren, let's praise Him, ___ and Him ___ a - lone. ___

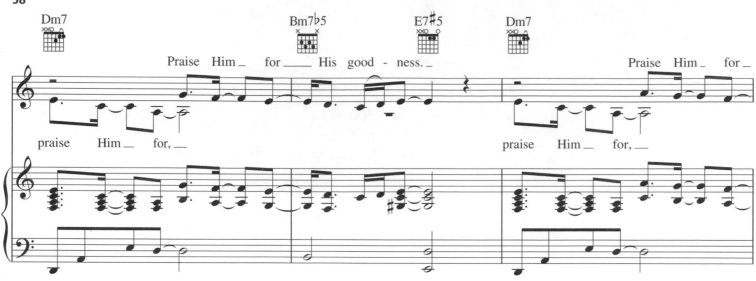

lu - jah is the high - est praise. _ Hal - le - lu - jah is the high - est praise, _ hal - le -

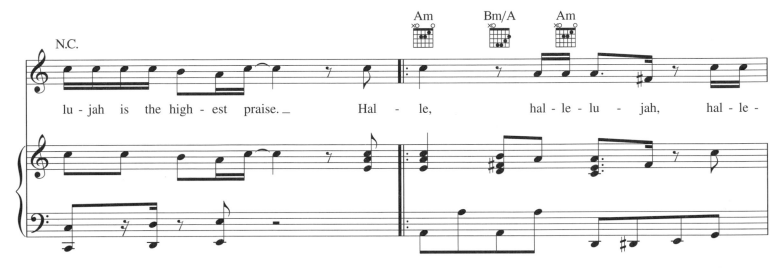

lu - jah is the high - est praise. _ Hal - le, hal - le - lu - jah, hal - le -

lu - jah is the high - est praise. _ Hal - le, hal - le - lu - jah, hal - le -

lu - jah is the high - est praise. _ Hal - lu - jah is the high - est praise. _ Throw up my

hands, raise my voice, move my feet, I will re-

joice. Throw up my hands, raise my voice, move my feet,

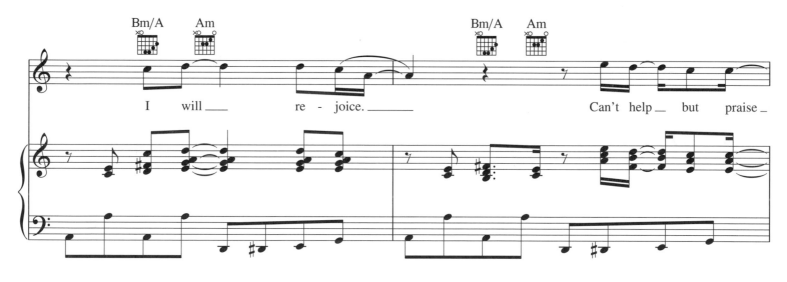

I will __ re - joice. __ Can't help __ but praise __

__ Him. Can't help __ but praise __ Him. Can't help __ but praise __

_____ Him. Can't help ___ but praise ___ Him. Move _____ and let ___ me praise ___

_____ Him, let ___ me praise ___ Him, let ___ me praise ___

_____ Him. Move _____ and let ___ me praise ___ Him. So raise your

hands, move side to side. Give up the praise, let God a -

rise. _____ Can't help _ but praise ___ Him. Can't help _ but praise _

_____ Him. Can't help _ but praise ___ Him. Can't help _ but praise _

_____ Him. So raise your _____ Him.

Move _____ and let _____ me praise ___ Him.

HEAVEN

Words and Music by ERICA ATKINS-CAMPBELL,
TRECINA ATKINS-CAMPBELL, JOI CAMPBELL,
WARRYN CAMPBELL, GENERAL JOHNSON,
GREGORY PERRY and BARNEY PERKINS

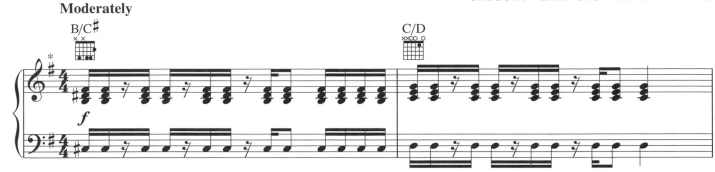

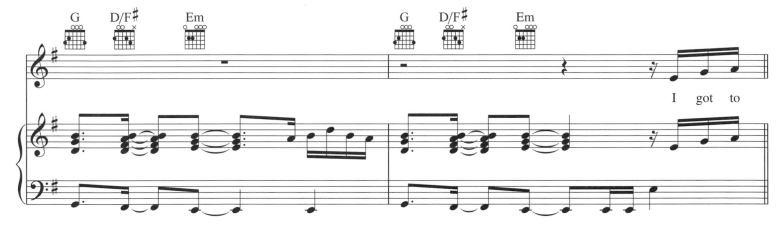

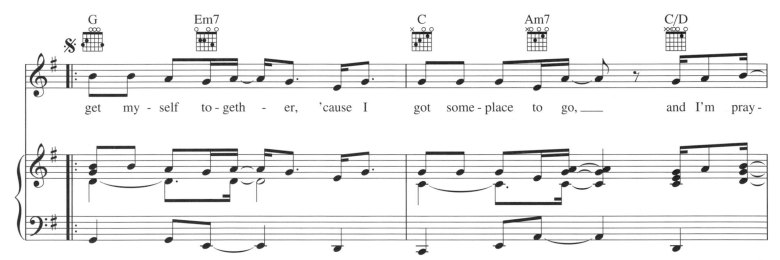

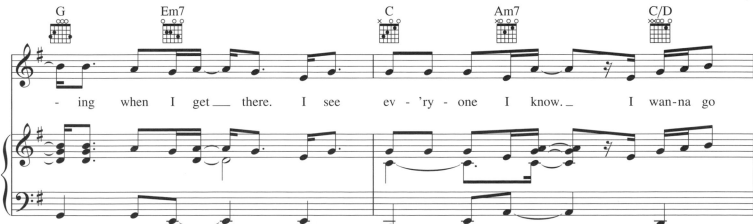

get my-self to-geth-er, 'cause I got some-place to go, ___ and I'm pray-
-ing when I get __ there. I see ev-'ry-one I know. _ I wan-na go

Recorded a half step lower.

it there _ some - day, _ I know. _

D.S. al Coda

I got to

CODA

(There's a

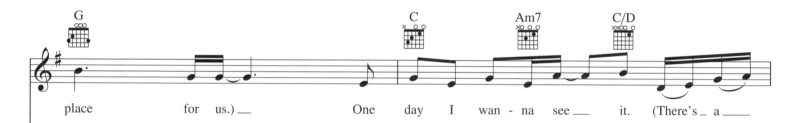

place for us.) _ One day I wan - na see _ it. (There's _ a _

place for us), _ and you may not be - lieve _ it, but I'm _

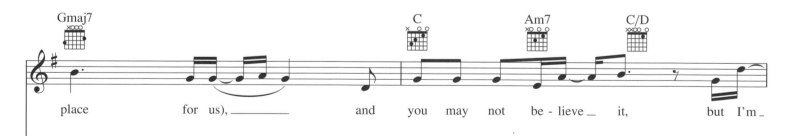

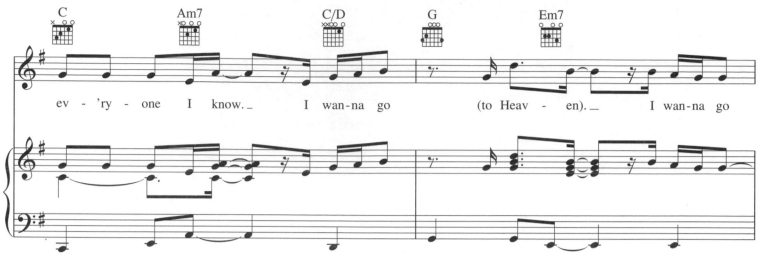

ev - 'ry - one I know.__ I wan-na go (to Heav - en).__ I wan-na go

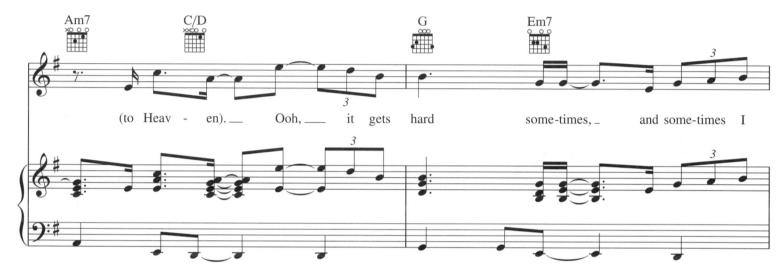

(to Heav - en).__ Ooh,__ it gets hard some-times,_ and some-times I

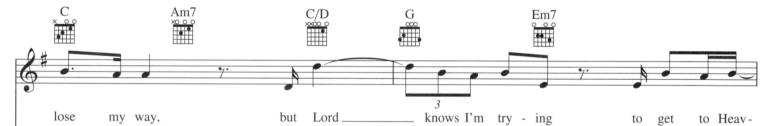

lose my way, but Lord _____ knows I'm try - ing to get to Heav-

- en some - day. Said I wan-na go (to Heav - en).__ I wan-na go

(to Heav - en). __ {Do you wan - na go (to Heav - en)? __ I wan - na go
Do you wan - na go?

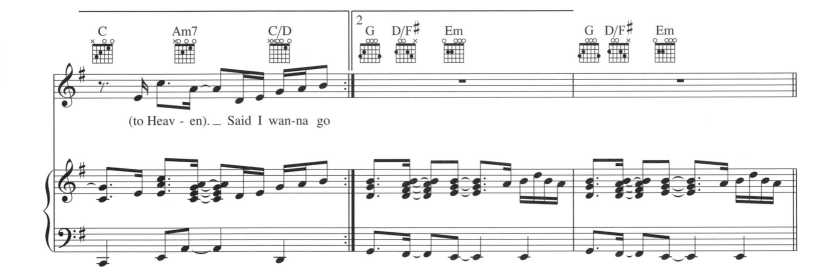

(to Heav - en). __ Said I wan-na go

Repeat and Fade   **Optional Ending**

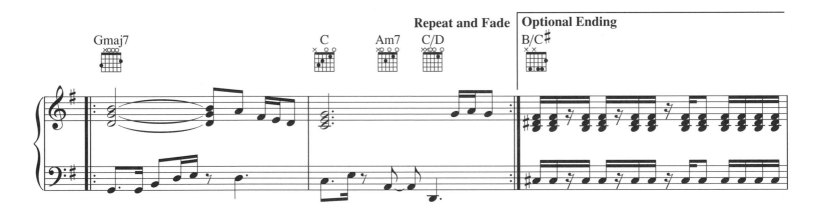

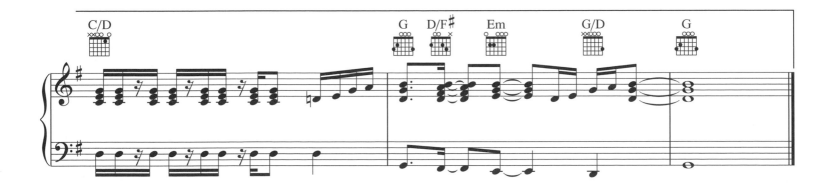

I NEED AN ANGEL

Words and Music by
R. KELLY

Moderately, in 1

I've run out of an-swers, __ I've run out of time, and
car-ry-ing a load that's __ too heav-y for me. Have

I'm so con-fused __ that I'm los-ing my mind. It's
no-where to go, __ so I'm down on my knees. I'm

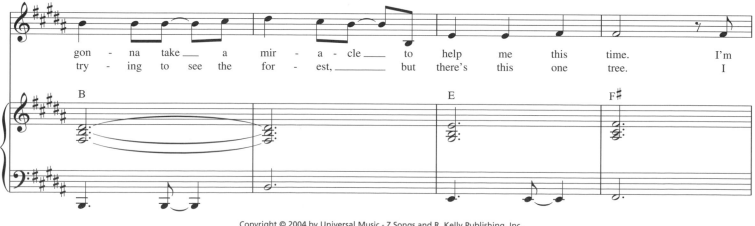

gon-na take __ a mir-a-cle __ to help me this time. I'm
try-ing to see the for-est, __ but there's this one tree. I

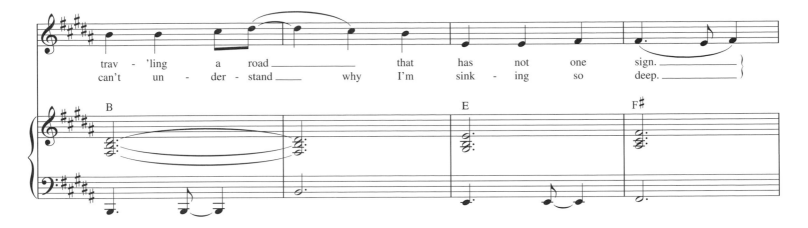

trav - 'ling a road _____ that has not one sign. _____
can't un - der - stand _____ why I'm sink - ing so deep. _____

B   E   F#

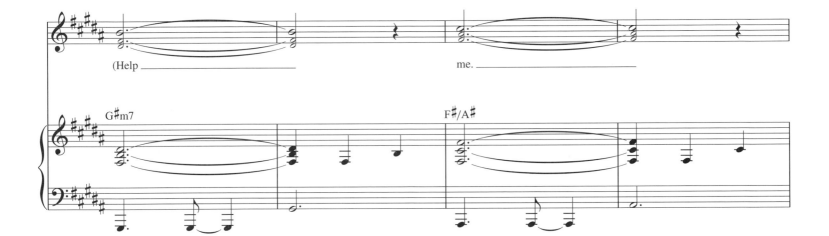

(Help _____ me. _____)

G#m7   F#/A#

Have mer - cy on

E/B   B   F#/A#

me.)   Set my soul _____ free _____

G#m7   F#/A#

and let the bell in my heart _____ ring.

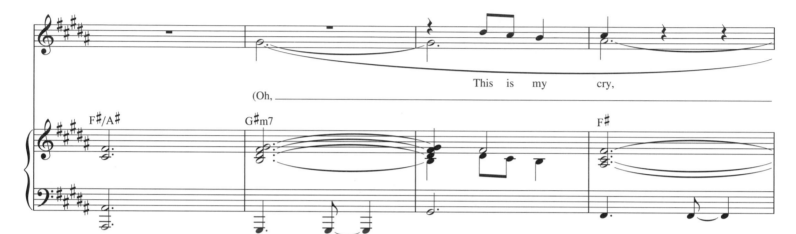

(Oh, _____ This is my cry,

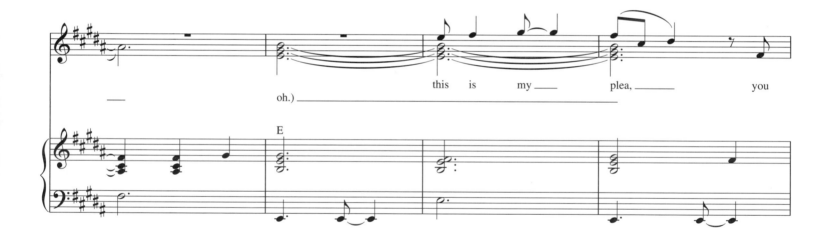

___ oh.) _____ this is my ___ plea, _____ you

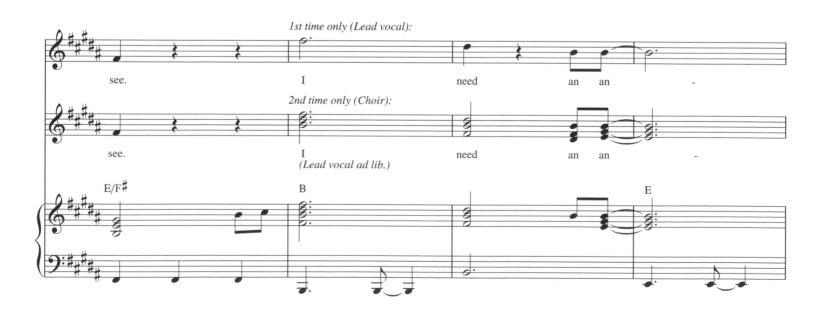

see. I need an an -

1st time only (Lead vocal):

see. I need an an -

2nd time only (Choir):

(Lead vocal ad lib.)

gel.   I'm   call   ing _____   an   an -

gel.   Call   ing   an   an -

F#   B   E

gel.   Send   me   an   an -

gel.   Send   me   an   an -

F#   B   E

gel _____   down. _____

gel _____   down. _____

F#   G#m7   E

74

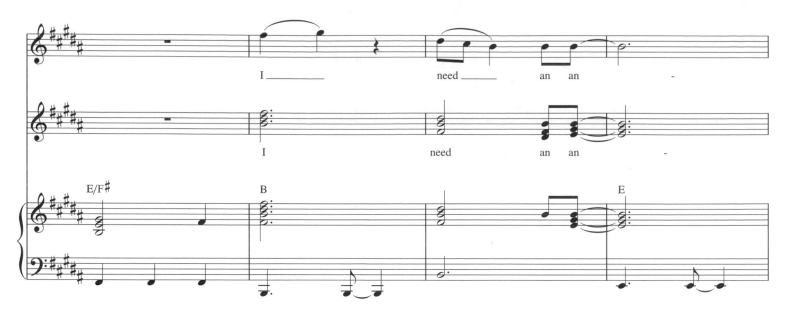

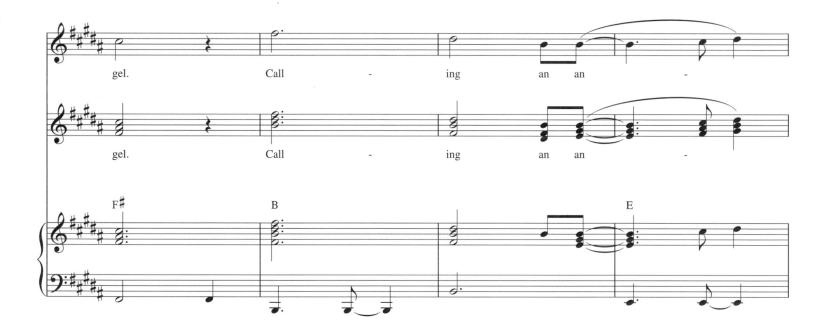

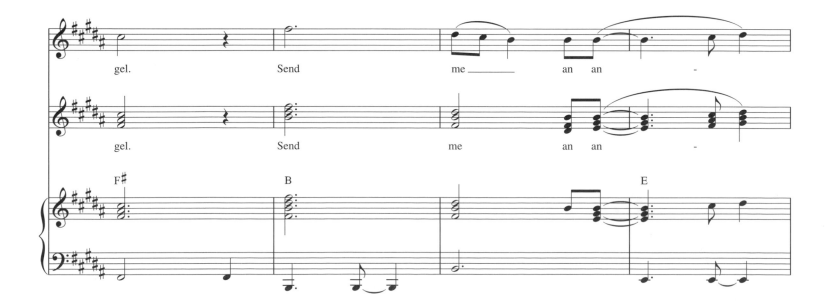

face _____ the truth, _____ so we run. _____ (Dah.)
(Dah.)

B/D#

(Dah.) God, if You care at all, _____ please don't
(Dah.)

E

let me fall _____ by the way - side. _____
(Dah.) (Dah.)

B/D#

(Dah.) Please be my Guide; _____

C#m7

would You light my path? _____ Take me, shape me,

Choir: Take me, shape me,

F#9sus

mold me, change me, teach me, fill me,

mold me, change me, teach me, fill me,

G9sus   G#9sus

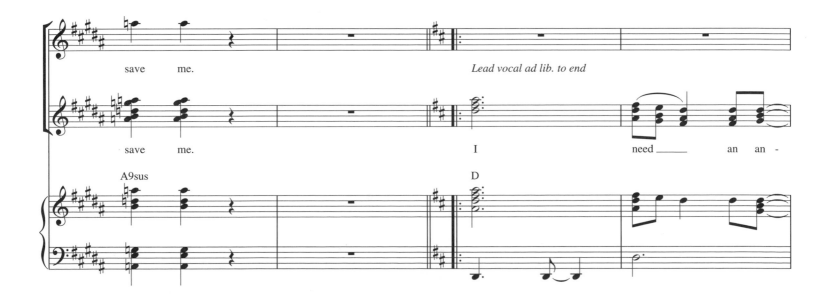

save me.   *Lead vocal ad lib. to end*

save me.   I   need _____ an an -

A9sus   D

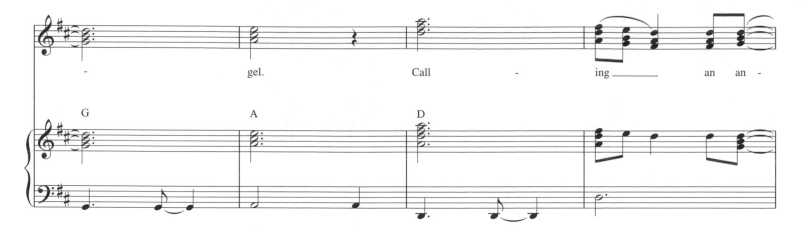

- gel. Call - ing _____ an an -

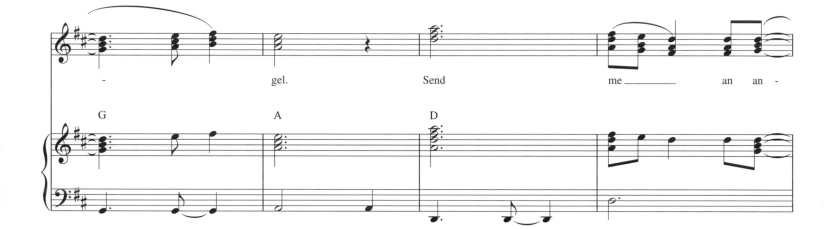

- gel. Send me _____ an an -

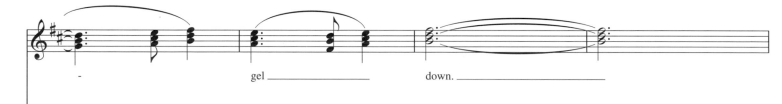

- gel _____ down. _____

Repeat and Fade | **Optional Ending**

Oh, _____

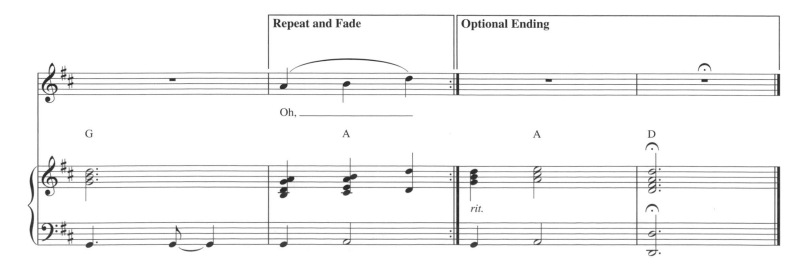

rit.

MIGHTY WIND

Words and Music by
ANDRAÉ CROUCH

Moderate Gospel Ballad

* Recorded a half step higher.

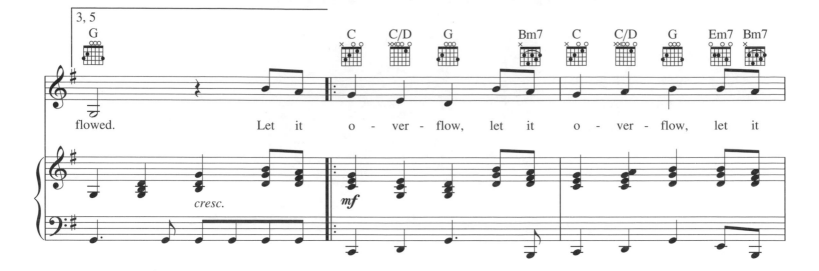

flowed. Let it o - ver - flow, let it o - ver - flow, let it

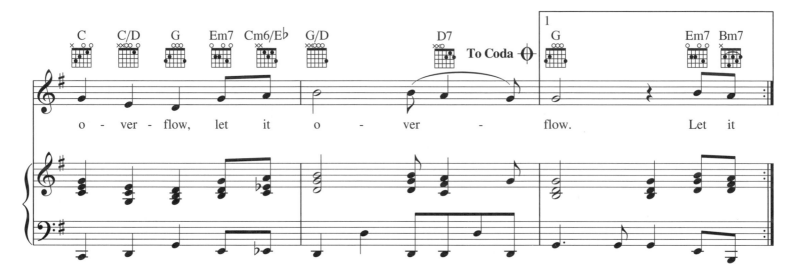

o - ver - flow, let it o - ver - flow. Let it

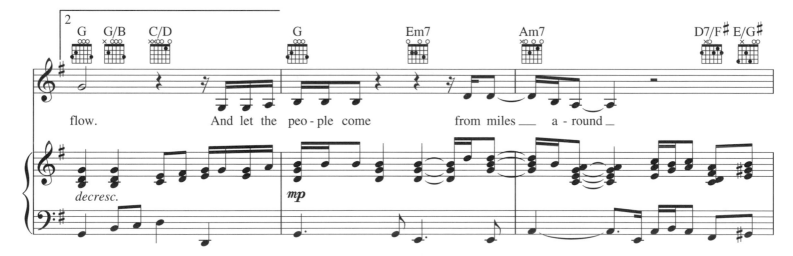

flow. And let the peo - ple come from miles _ a - round _

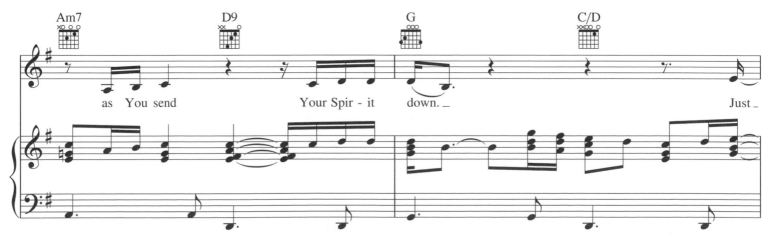

as You send Your Spir - it down. _ Just _

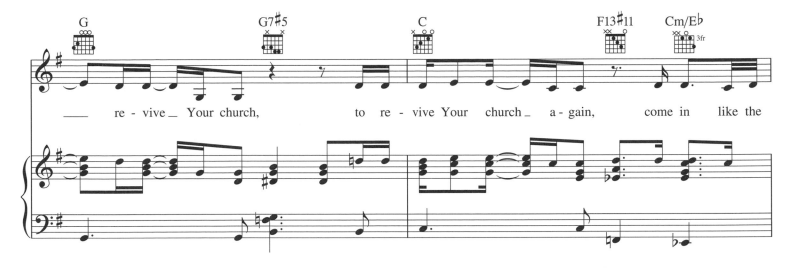

re - vive __ Your church, to re - vive Your church __ a - gain, come in like the

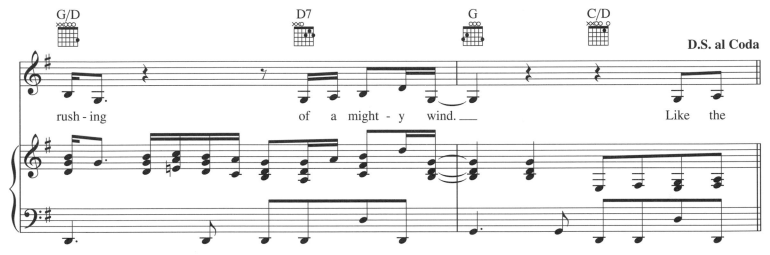

rush - ing of a might - y wind. __ Like the

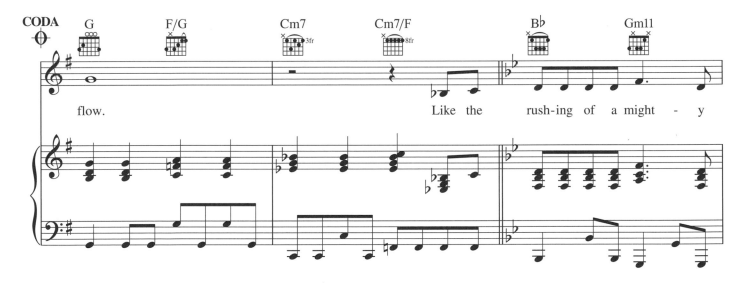

CODA

flow. Like the rush - ing of a might - y

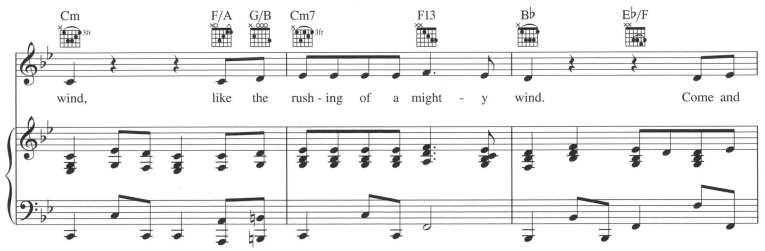

wind, like the rush - ing of a might - y wind. Come and

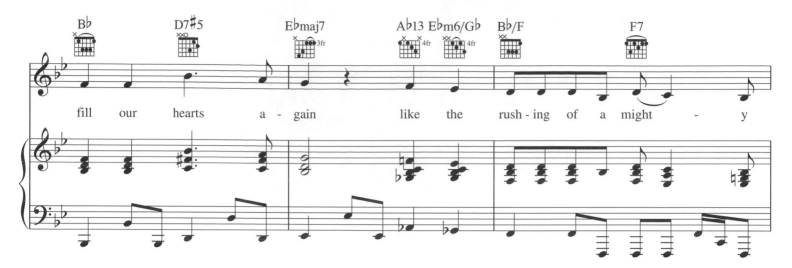

fill our hearts a - gain like the rush - ing of a might - y

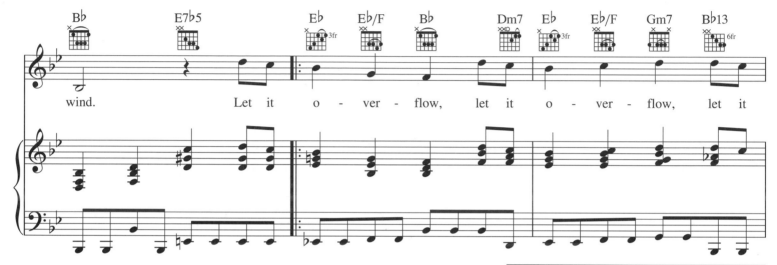

wind. Let it o - ver - flow, let it o - ver - flow, let it

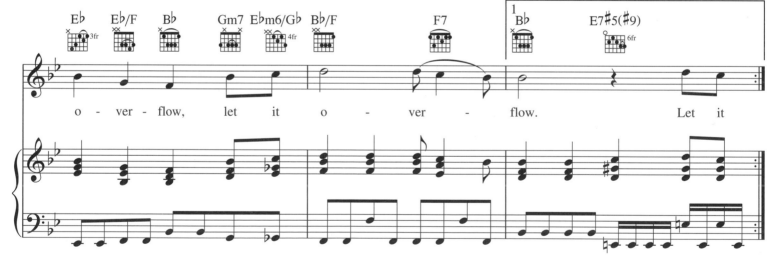

o - ver - flow, let it o - ver - flow. Let it

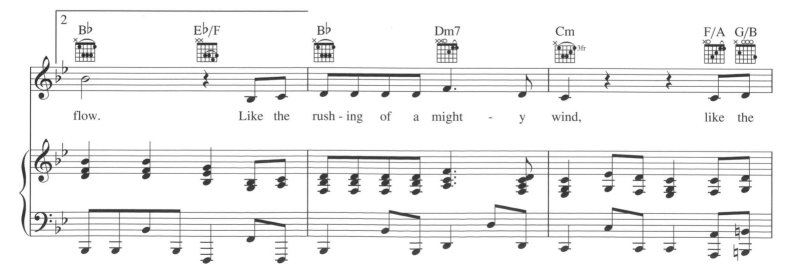

flow. Like the rush - ing of a might - y wind, like the

rush - ing of a might - y wind. Come and fill our hearts a -

gain like the rush - ing of a might - y wind. Like the

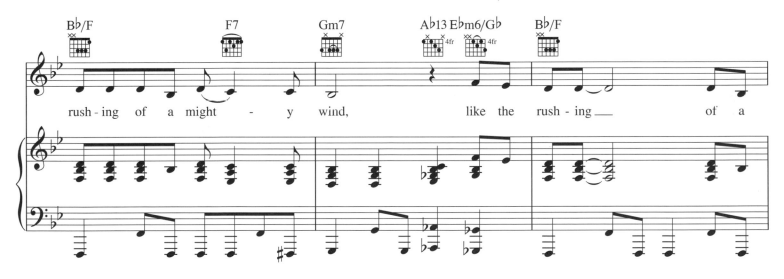

rush - ing of a might - y wind, like the rush - ing____ of a

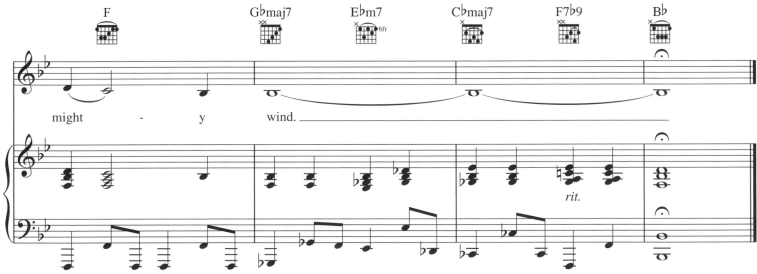

might - y wind. _____

I NEED YOU NOW

Words and Music by
SMOKIE NORFUL

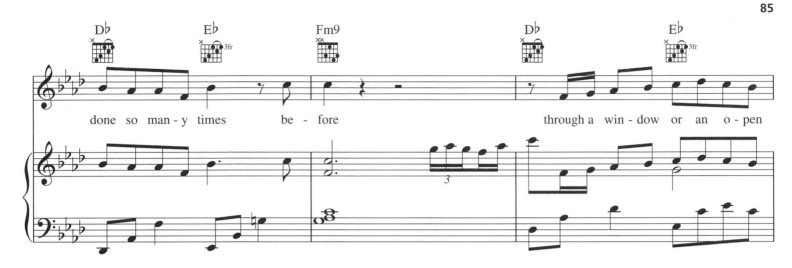

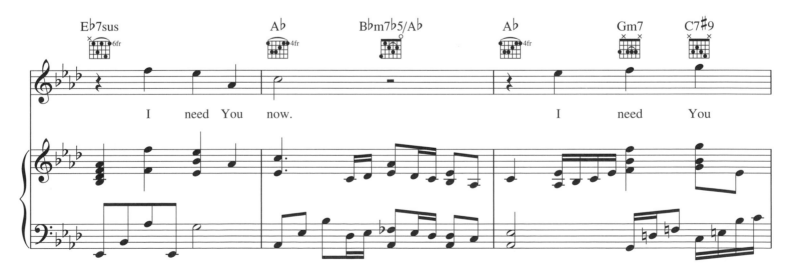

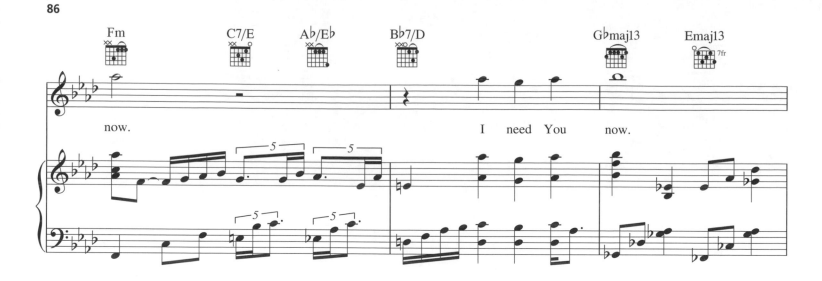

now.   I need You   now.

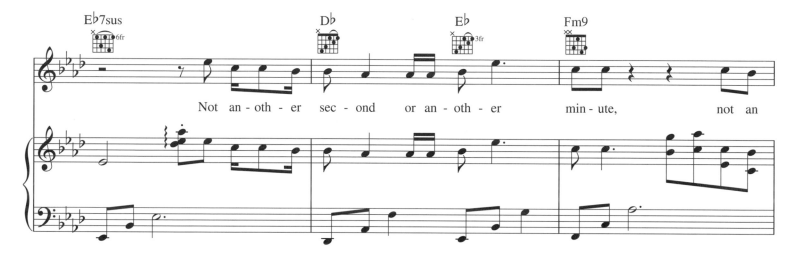

Not an - oth - er sec - ond   or an - oth - er   min - ute,   not an

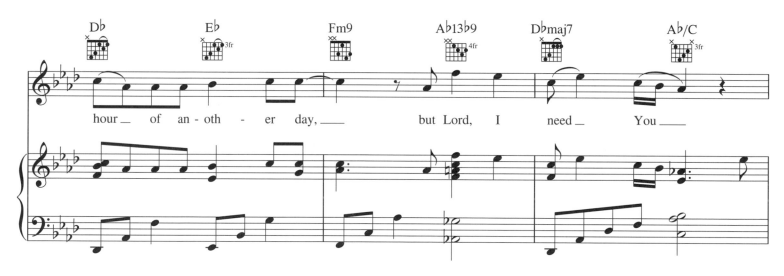

hour __ of an - oth - er day, ___   but Lord, I   need __ You ___

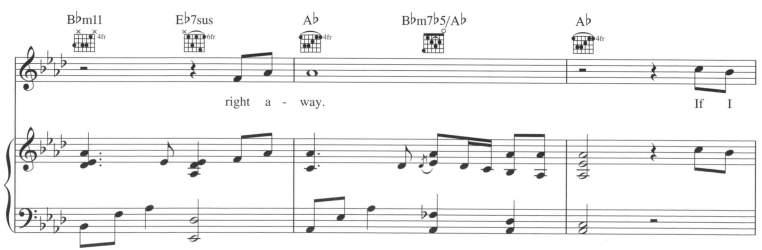

right a - way.   If I

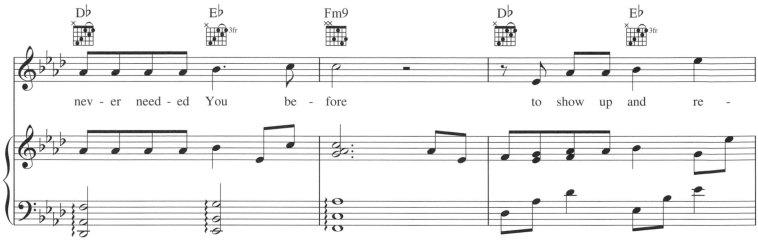

never need-ed You be-fore to show up and re-

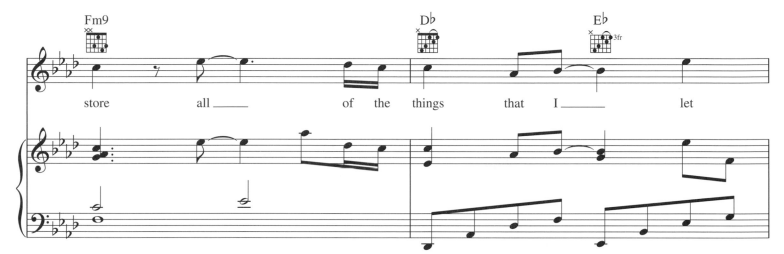

store all _____ of the things that I _____ let

slip while I was yet search-ing the world __

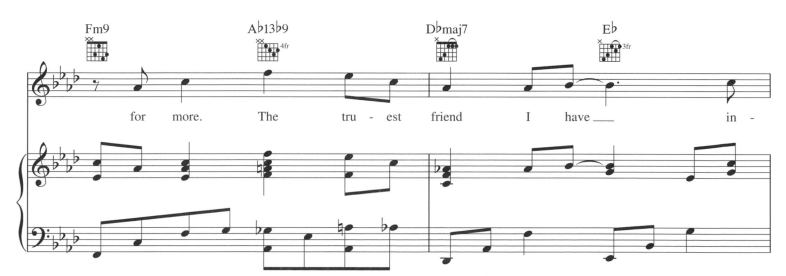

for more. The tru-est friend I have _____ in-

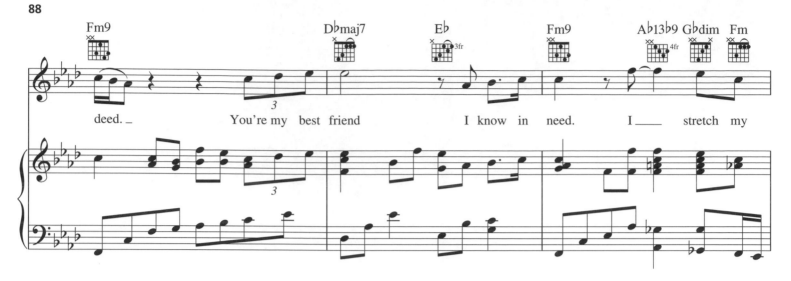

deed. _ You're my best friend I know in need. I ___ stretch my

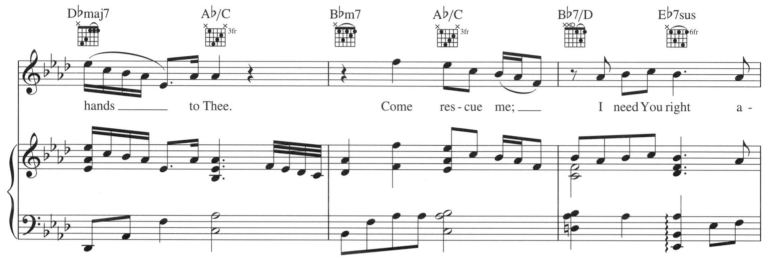

hands _____ to Thee. Come res-cue me; ___ I need You right a-

way. _____ The ag-o-ny of be-ing a-lone, ___

the fear of do-ing things on my own, the tests and tri-als that

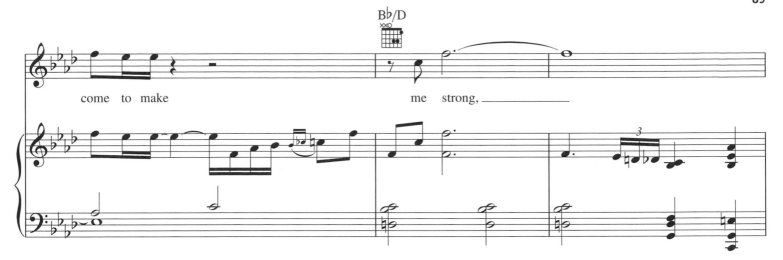

come to make me strong, _____

the feel - ings of guilt, hurt, __ shame __ and de - feat,

the waves of tri - als that feed up - on _____ me,

but to know, Lord, _____ that in You I've got vic - to - ry. _____

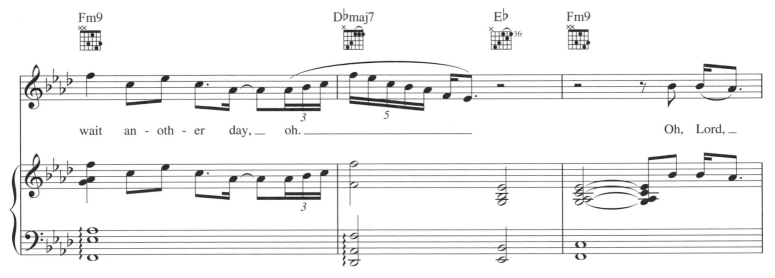

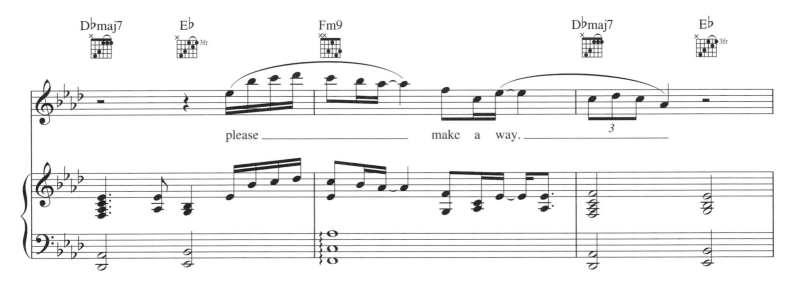

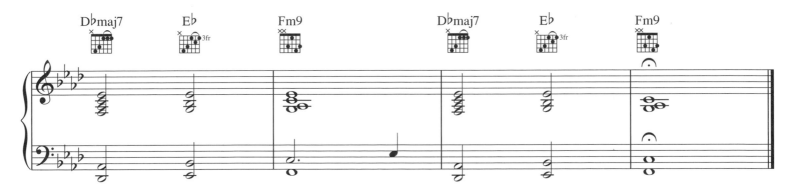

I'LL TRUST YOU

Words and Music by
RICHARD SMALLWOOD

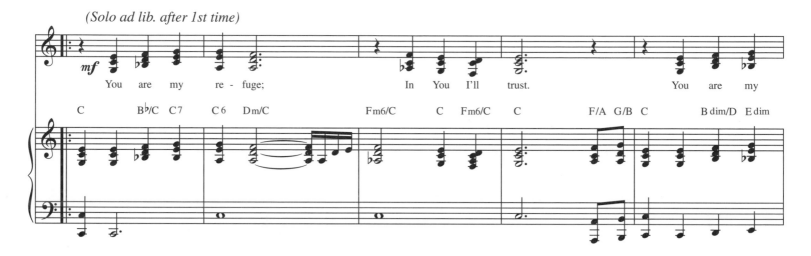

Your shad - ow. I won't dread___ the ter-ror by night, for an-gels are all___ a -

round me. So___ I will___ not fear.

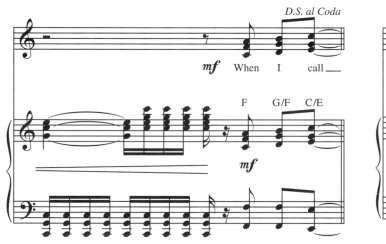

D.S. al Coda
When I call___ I'll trust___ You,___ for I___ will dwell un - der

Coda
dwell un - der Your shad - ow.

dwell un - der Your shad - ow.

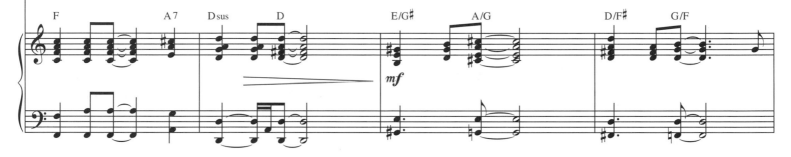

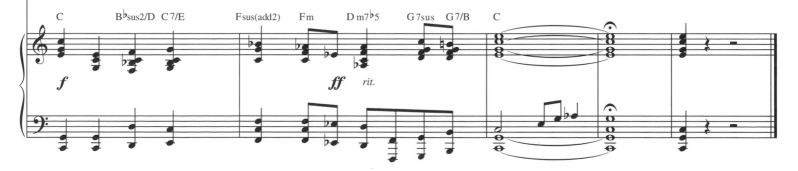

IMAGINE ME

Words and Music by
KIRK FRANKLIN

I - mag - ine me __ be - ing free, __ trust - ing You __ to - tal - ly. __

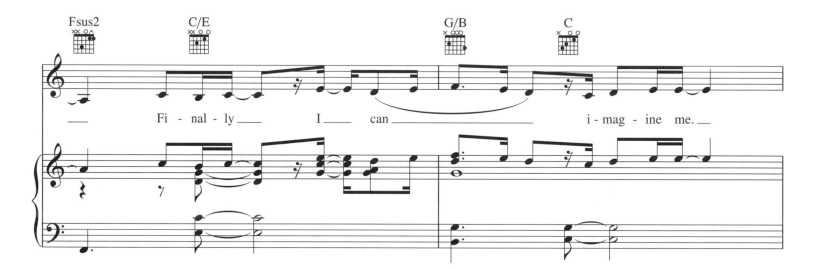

__ Fi - nal - ly __ I __ can __ i - mag - ine me. __

I __ ad - mit __ it was hard to see, __ You be - ing in love __ with some - one like me, __

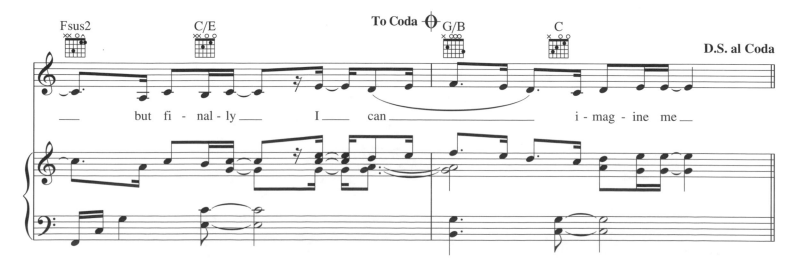

__ but fi - nal - ly __ I __ can __ i - mag - ine me __

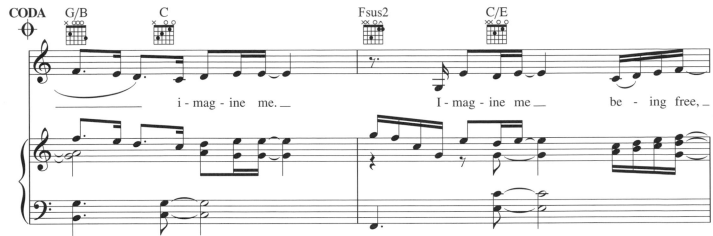

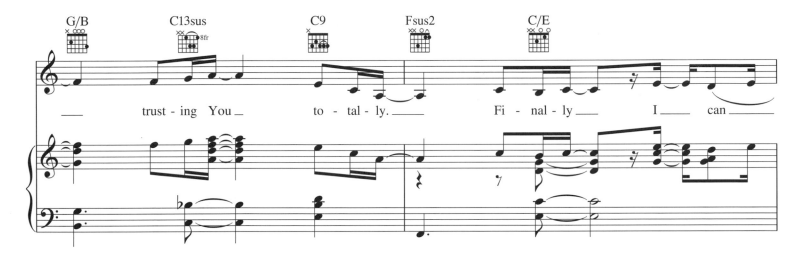

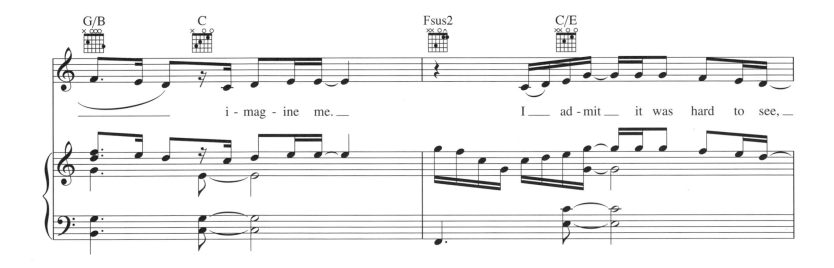

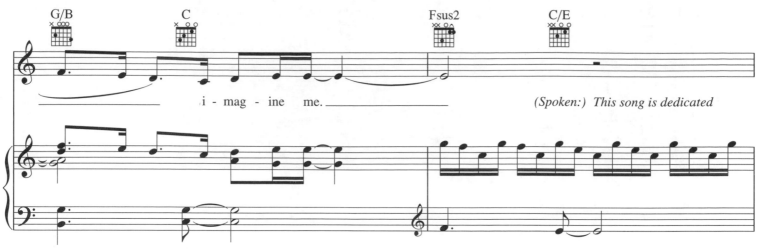

i - mag - ine me. _____ *(Spoken:) This song is dedicated*

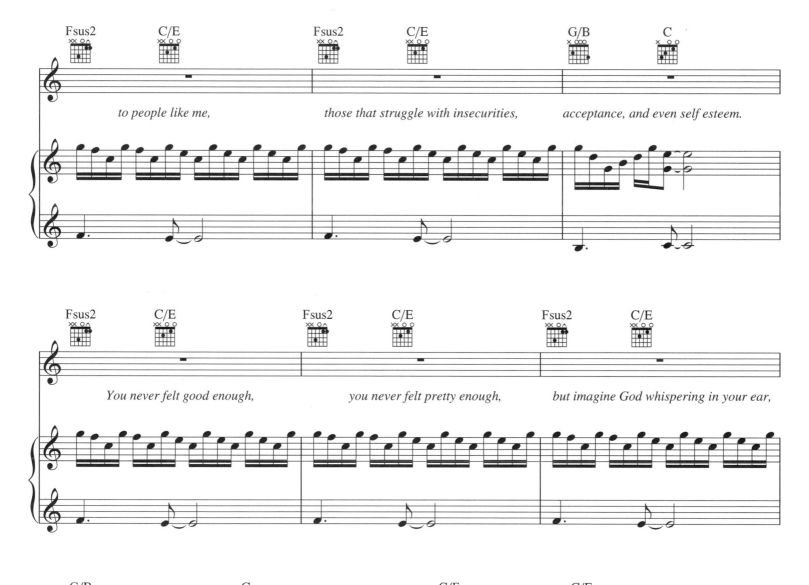

to people like me,   *those that struggle with insecurities,*   *acceptance, and even self esteem.*

You never felt good enough,   *you never felt pretty enough,*   *but imagine God whispering in your ear,*

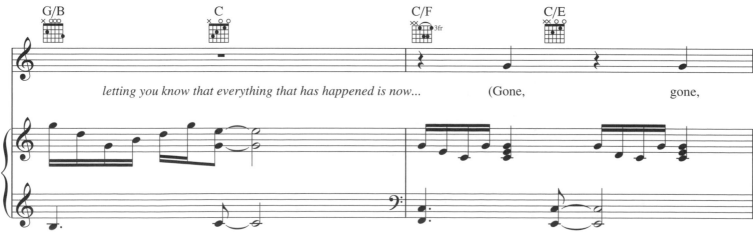

letting you know that everything that has happened is now...   (Gone,   gone,

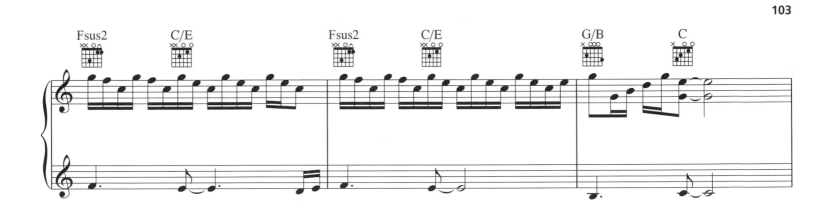

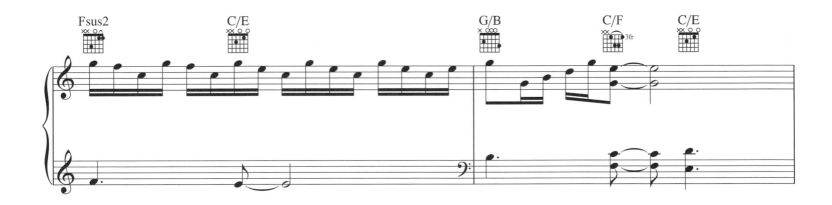

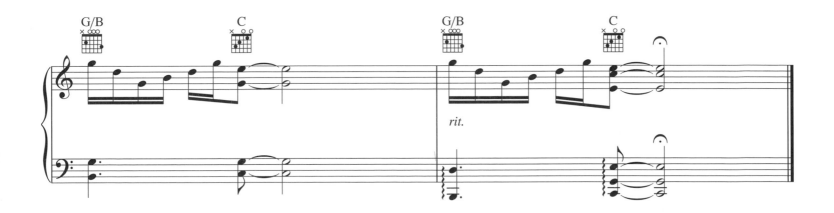

IN YOUR NAME

Words and Music by
JOHN P. KEE

that ___ I'll heed ___ to ___ Your call. ___ It's in ___ Your name ___
that ___ I shall ___ talk ___ the talk. ___ By ___ Your Word ___

B♭m7　　B♭/D　　E♭　　D♭13♯11

___ that ___ all pow - er ___ is giv - en. ___ I have au -
___ I'm ___ a - noint - ed and I'm called. ___

A♭/C　　B♭m7　　A♭　　G♭7　　F　E♭7/G　F/A

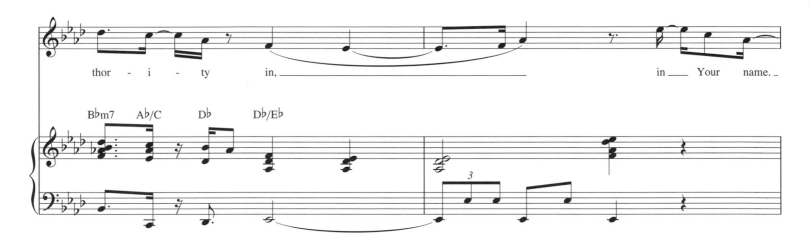

thor - i - ty in, ___ in ___ Your name. ___

B♭m7　A♭/C　　D♭　　D♭/E♭

Ooh, ___　　ooh, ___　　ooh, ___

G♭/A♭　　D♭/A♭　　D♭m6/A♭　　A♭　　G♭/A♭　　D♭/A♭

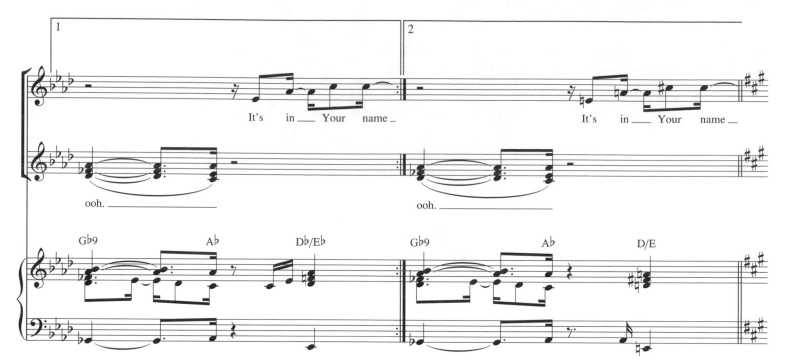

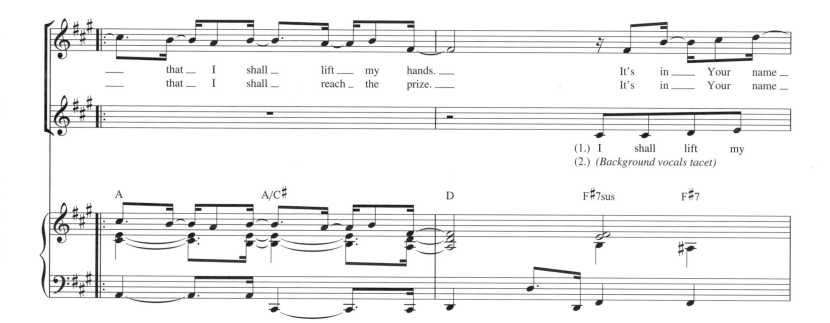

It's in ___ Your name ___ that ___ I shall ___ reach ___ my goal. ___

ooh. ___

It's in ___ Your name ___ that ___ I shall ___ win ___ a soul. ___

It's in ___ Your name ___ that ___ Your Word ___ shall ne'er ___ wax

cold. ___ I have au - thor - i - ty in, ___

in ___ Your name. ___

Ooh, ___

It's in Your

ooh, ___ ooh, ___ ooh. ___

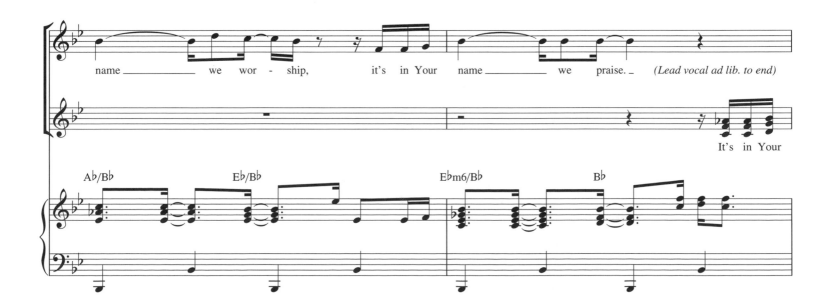

name ___ we wor - ship, it's in Your name ___ we praise. _ *(Lead vocal ad lib. to end)*

It's in Your

name _____ we wor - ship, in ___ Your name _____ we praise. ___ It's in Your

A♭/B♭   E♭/B♭   E♭m6/B♭   B♭

name _____ we wor - ship, in ___ Your name _____ we praise. ___ It's in Your

Fm9   E♭/B♭   E♭m6/B♭   B♭

name _____ we wor - ship, in ___ Your name _____ we praise. ___

A♭/B♭   E♭/B♭   E♭m6/B♭   B♭

Lord, to - day ___ I wor - ship You. ___ I give You hon - or, I give ___ You praise. ___

Fm9   E♭/B♭   E♭m6   B♭

name _____ we wor - ship, in ___ Your name _____ we praise. ___ It's in Your

A♭/B♭ E♭/B♭ E♭m6/B♭ B♭

name _____ we wor - ship, in ___ Your name _____ we praise. ___ It's in Your

A♭/B♭ E♭/B♭ E♭m6/B♭ B♭

name _____ we wor - ship, in ___ Your name _____ we praise. ___

Fm9 E♭/B♭ E♭m6 B♭

Lord, to - day ___ I wor - ship You. ___ I give You hon - or, I give ___ You praise. ___

A♭/B♭ E♭/B♭ E♭m6/B♭ B♭

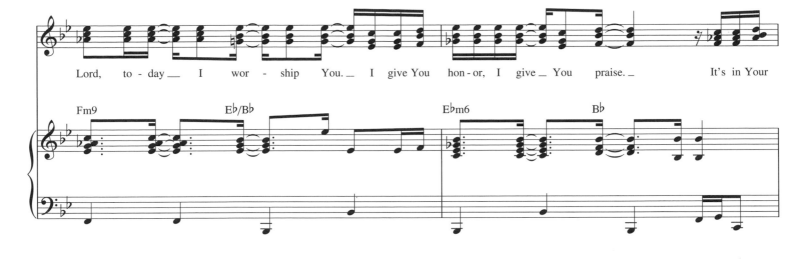

Lord, to-day __ I wor - ship You. __ I give You hon - or, I give __ You praise. __ It's in Your

name _____ we wor - ship, in __ Your name _____ we praise. __

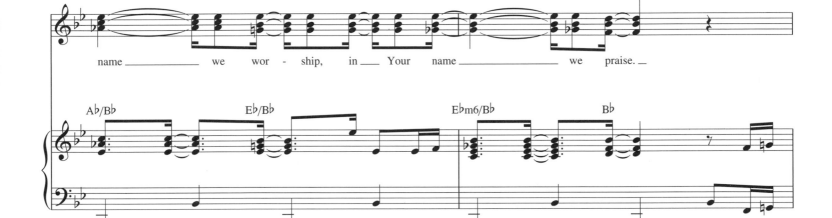

LOOK AT ME NOW

Words and Music by
KIRK FRANKLIN

Per-se-cut-ed, crit-i-cized, ____ been de-nied ____ and a-ban-

doned. Pushed a-way, giv-en a-way, ____ some days I could-n't i-mag-

ine. Get-tin' hot-ter, get-tin' cold-er. What's hard for me to see. ____

Tired of run-ning, tired of hurt - ing, e - ven got tired of me. Tired of cry - ing, tired of try -

ing to for-get my mis-takes. Tired of be - ing in the storm; __ how much more can I take?

Man - y nights in my life, tell me why I shed more tears my eyes __ would al - low. __

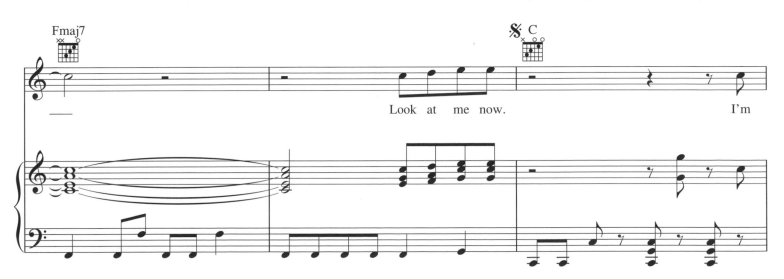

Look at me now. I'm

strong - er this time _ a - round, _ not be - cause I was so good, but some - how _

_ You looked past where I was, and You knew _

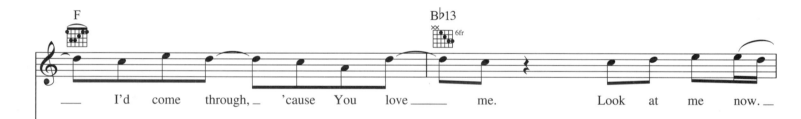

_ I'd come through, _ 'cause You love _____ me. Look at me now. _

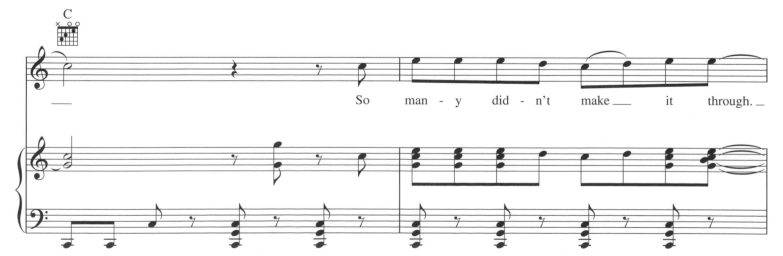

_ So man - y did - n't make ___ it through. _

That's why this heart be - longs to on - ly You.

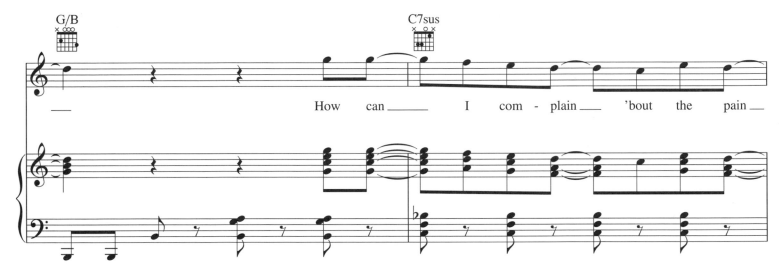

How can _____ I com - plain _____ 'bout the pain _____

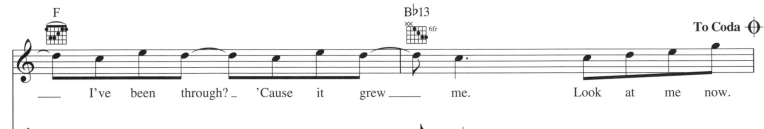

_____ I've been through? _ 'Cause it grew _____ me. Look at me now.

To Coda

Had no hope, had no fu - ture; e - ven too hard to dream. _ No one told me, "Boy, you can

be what-ev-er you wan-na be." Then You saved me and You gave me rea-son to breathe a-gain.

Not per-fect, yo, but I'm gon' run 'til I make it to the end. (It ain't eas-y when your life's _

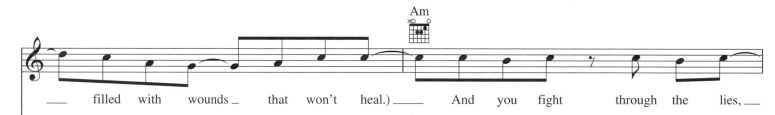

_ filled with wounds _ that won't heal.) _ And you fight through the lies, _

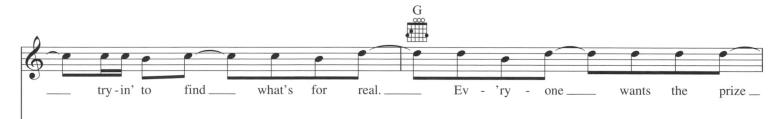

_ try-in' to find _ what's for real. _ Ev-'ry-one _ wants the prize _

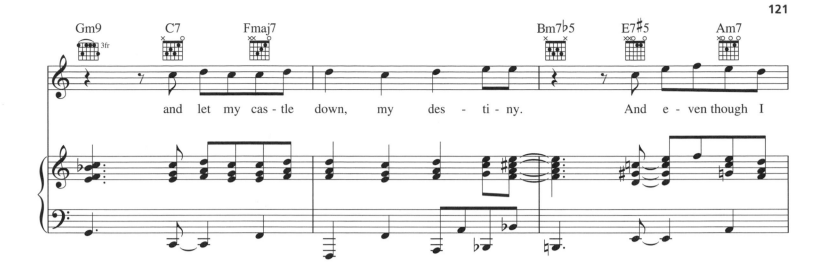

and let my cas-tle down, my des-ti-ny. And e-ven though I

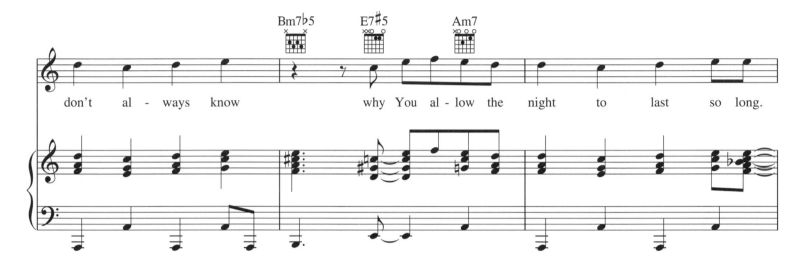

don't al-ways know why You al-low the night to last so long.

But when I see the sun-light, it was on-ly to make me strong.

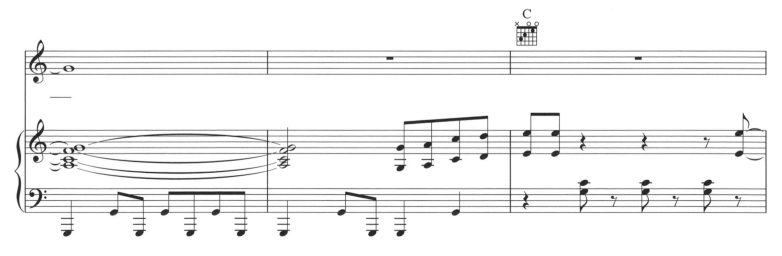

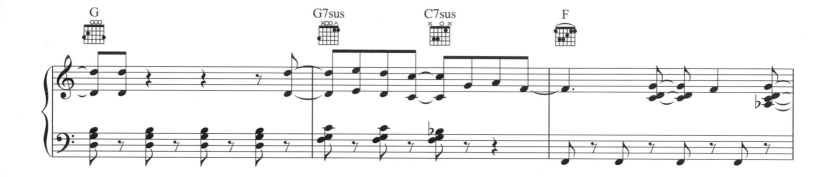

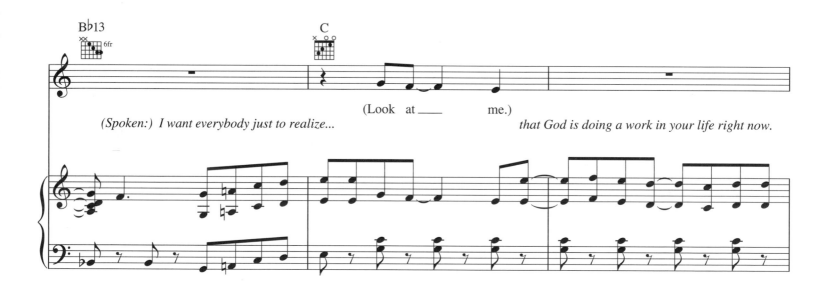

(Spoken:) I want everybody just to realize...
(Look at ___ me.)
that God is doing a work in your life right now.

(Look at ___ me.)
(Look at ___ me.)
I know it may not feel comfortable to you, but just remember...

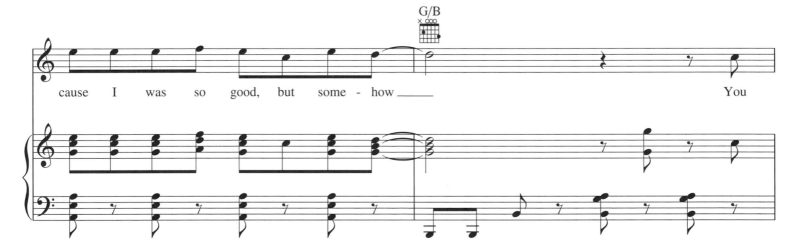

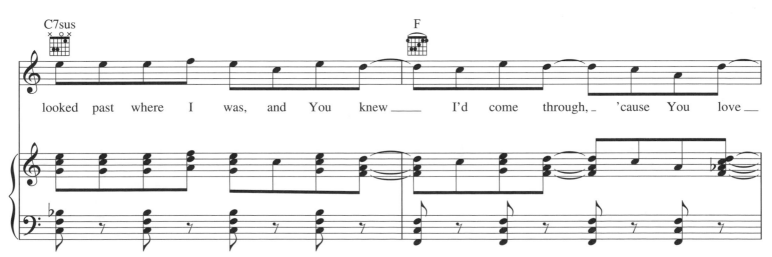

Bb13

C

(1.,3.) I'm bet - ter now.
(2.,4.) I'm strong - er now.

Am7

I'm clos - er now. I'm thank - ful now.
I'm pa - tient now. I'm grate - ful now.

G/B

C7sus

F

I'm hap - py now.
I'll praise You now.

Look at ___ me.

1-3
Fm6

Bb13

4
Fm6

Bb13

C

Look at ___ me.

Look at ___ me.

MY EVERYTHING

Words and Music by
RICHARD SMALLWOOD

Moderately slow, in 2

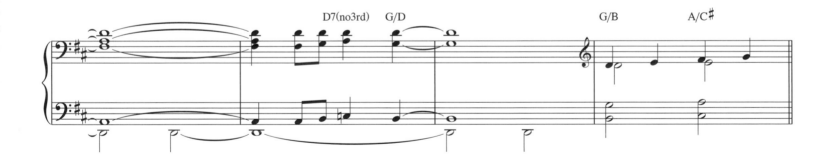

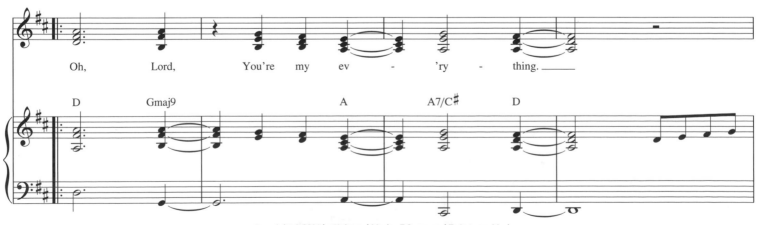

Oh, Lord, You're my ev - 'ry - thing. ____

Praise wait - eth for Thee, my King. Oh, _____ Thou _____

_____ who hear - est ev - 'ry prayer, _____

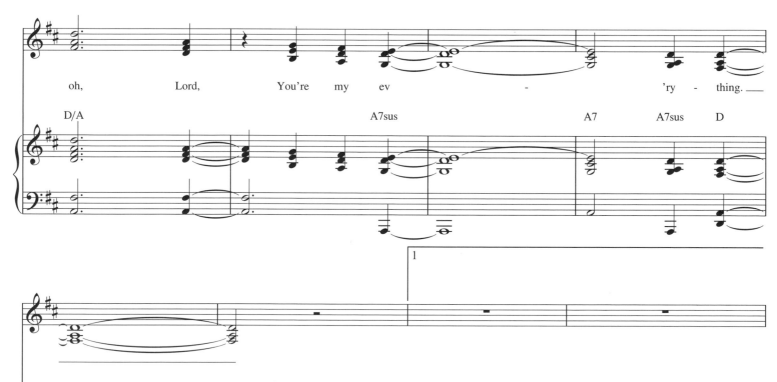

oh, Lord, You're my ev - 'ry - thing. _____

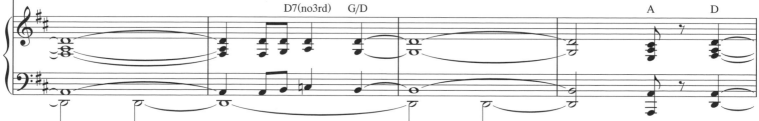

(Lead vocal ad lib. to end) You

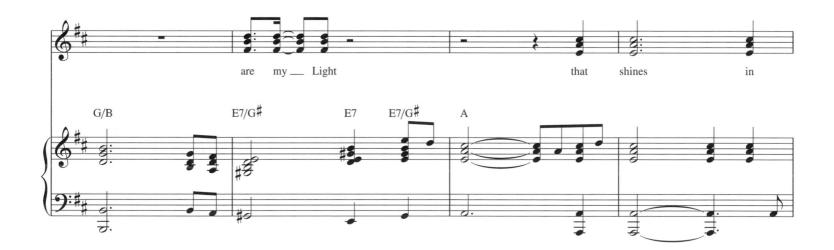

are my __ Light   that   shines   in

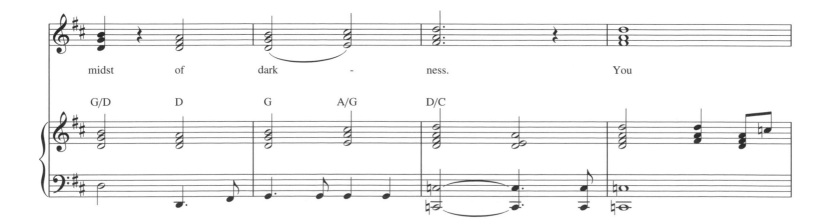

midst   of   dark   -   ness.   You

are my ___ Help; You're there in

time of trou - ble. Oh, where

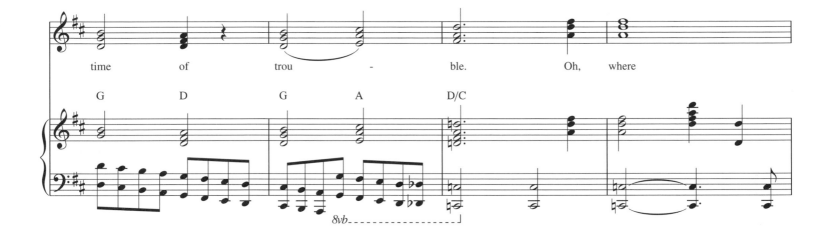

would I ___ be if not but

for Your mer - cy? Oh, Lord, You're my ev -

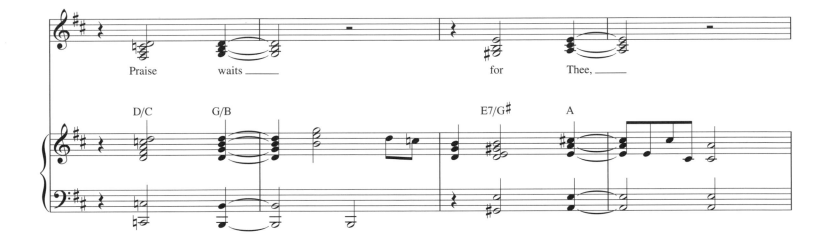

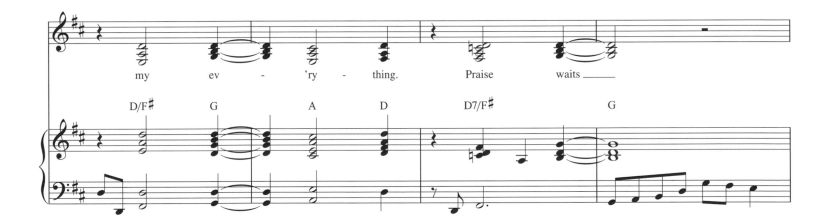

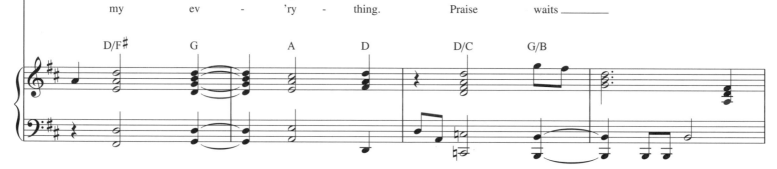

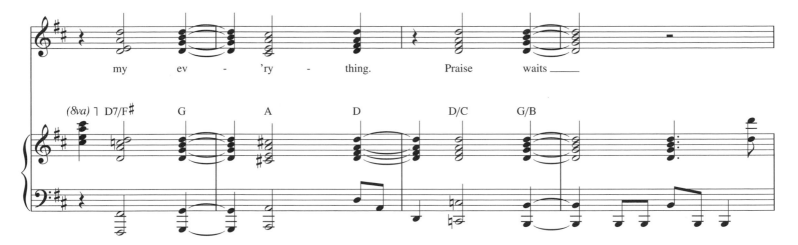

my ev - 'ry - thing. Praise waits _____

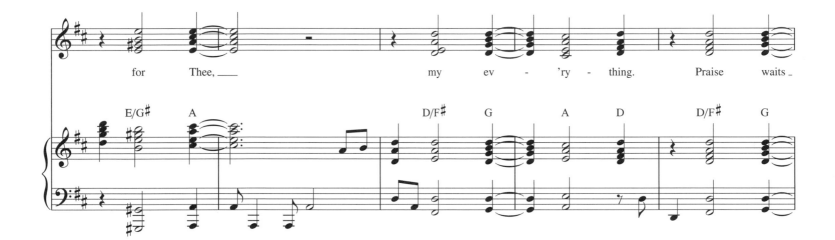

for Thee, _____ my ev - 'ry - thing. Praise waits ___

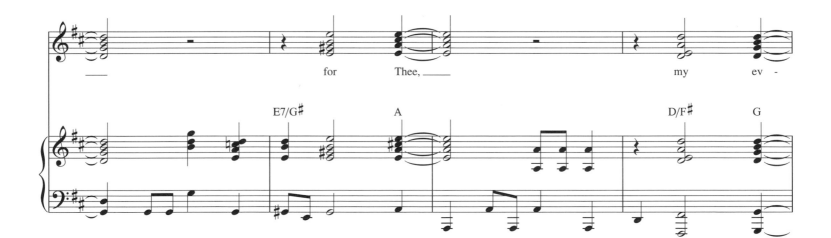

_____ for Thee, _____ my ev -

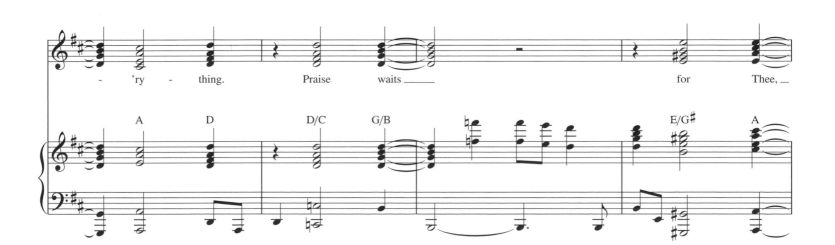

- 'ry - thing. Praise waits _____ for Thee, __

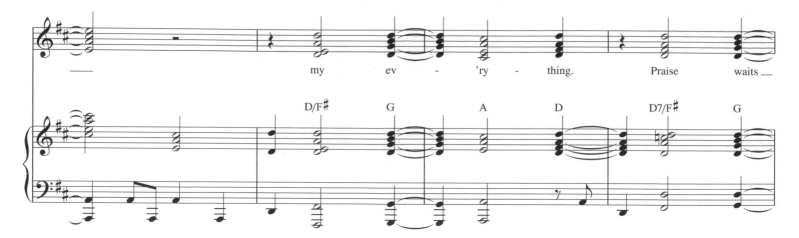

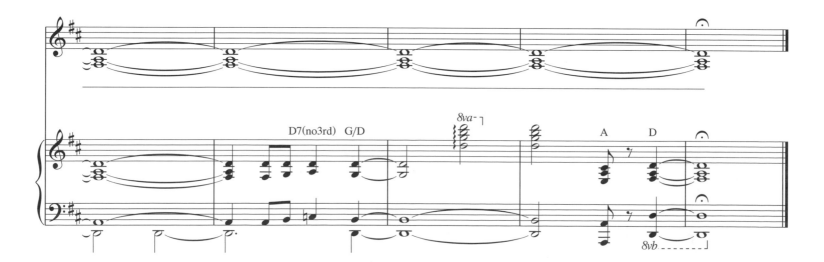

OPEN MY HEART

Words and Music by JAMES HARRIS III, TERRY LEWIS,
JAMES QUENTON and YOLANDA ADAMS

Very slowly

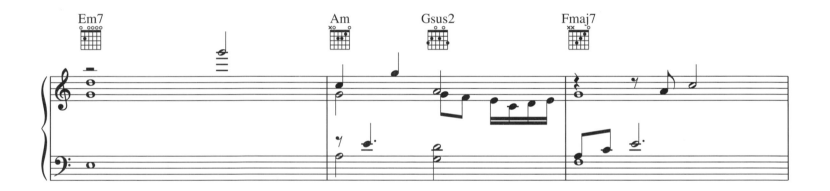

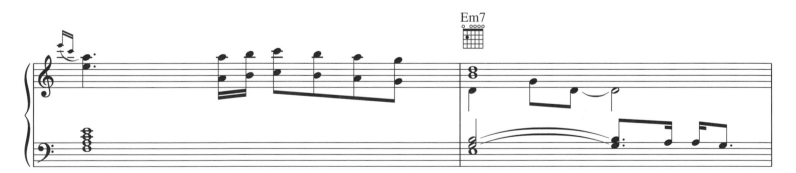

* Recorded a half step higher.

A-lone in a room

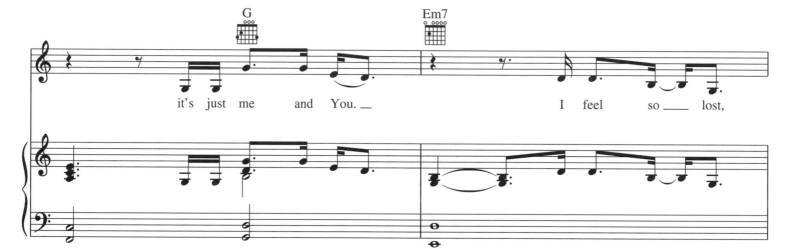

it's just me and You. __ I feel so __ lost,

'cause I don't know what to do. Now what if I chose __

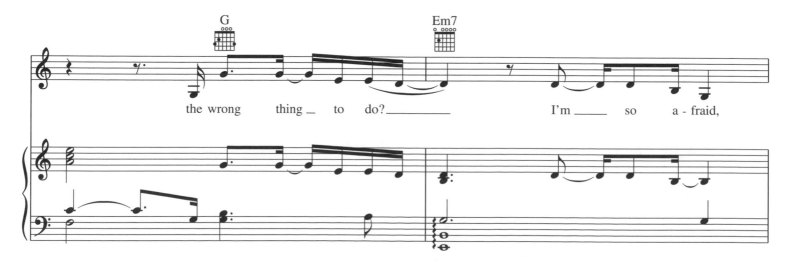

the wrong thing __ to do? _____ I'm __ so a-fraid,

ONLY YOU ARE HOLY

Words and Music by
DONNIE McCLURKIN

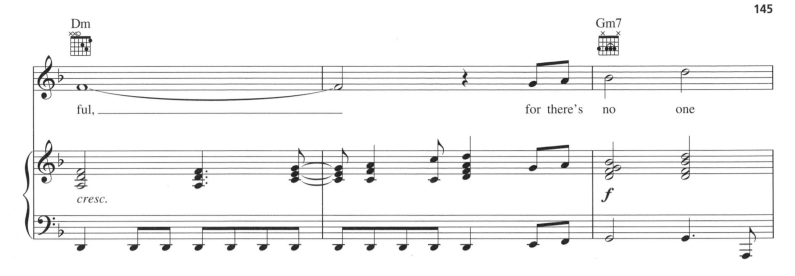

ful, _____ for there's no one

else like You _____ who is

faith - ful, ev - er true. _____

_____ All my love, my heart, my

SHACKLES
(Praise You)

Words and Music by WARRYN CAMPBELL,
ERICA ATKINS and TRECINA ATKINS

(Spoken:) Sure is hot out here.... ya know, I don't mind though.

Just glad to be free. Know what I'm sayin'? Take the

shack - les off my feet so I can dance. _ I just _ wan - na

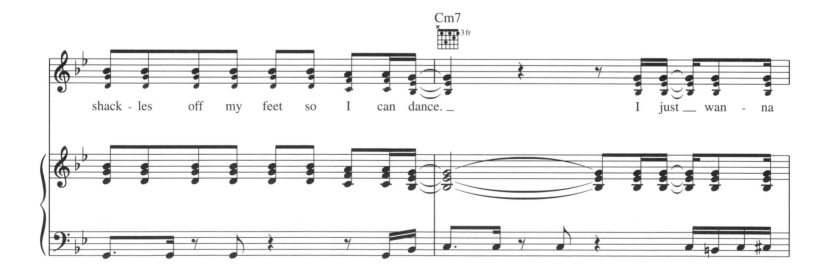

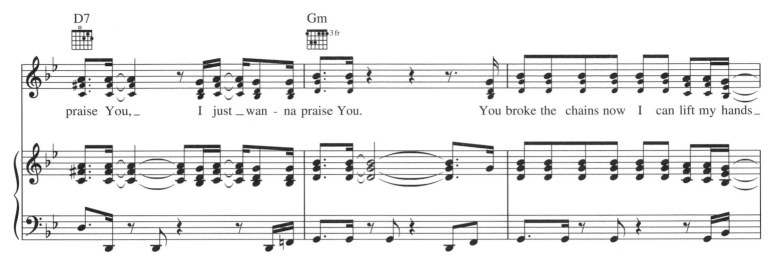

praise You,___ I just __ wan - na praise You. You broke the chains now I can lift my hands ___

___ and I'm _ gon - na praise You. _ I'm _ gon - na praise You. In the

cor - ners of __ my mind __ I just _ can't seem __ to find __ a rea - son to ___ be-lieve

that I ___ can break _____ free. 'Cause you __ see, I _____ been

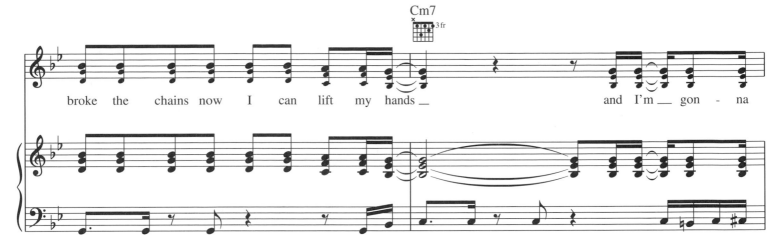

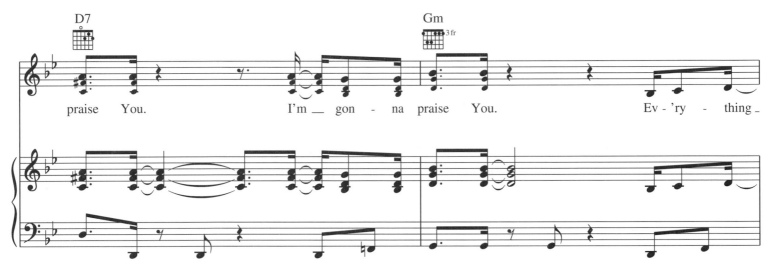

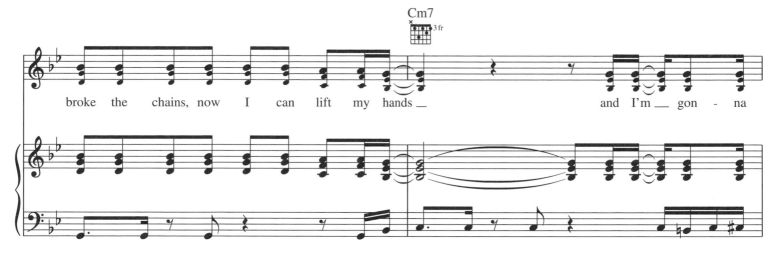

broke the chains, now I can lift my hands ___ and I'm ___ gon - na

praise You. ___ I'm ___ gon - na praise You. ___ Been ___

through the fi - re and ___ the rain, ___ bound in ev' - ry kind ___ of way. _____ But

God has bro - ken ev' - 'ry chain _____ so let me go ___ right _____ now. _____ Take the

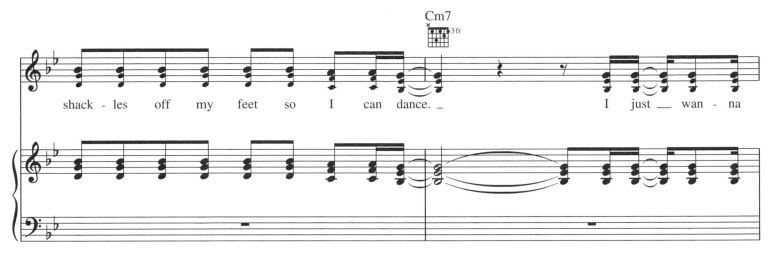

shack - les off my feet so I can dance. ___ I just ___ wan - na

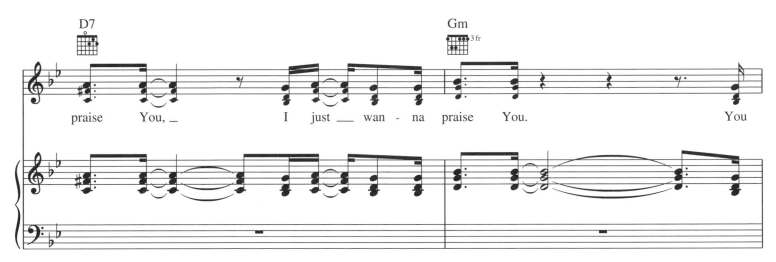

praise You, ___ I just ___ wan - na praise You. You

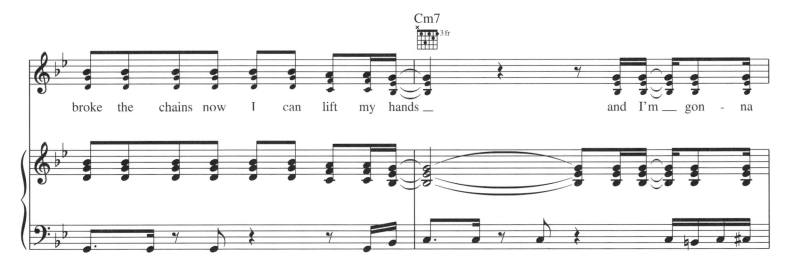

broke the chains now I can lift my hands ___ and I'm ___ gon - na

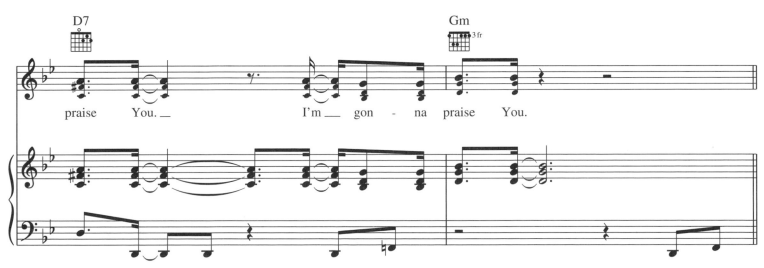

praise You. ___ I'm ___ gon - na praise You.

Repeat and Fade

Take 'em off.   Take 'em off.

What's ya' gon-na do?   Huh,   yeah,   your du-ty.   You

broke the chains now I can lift my hands __   and I'm __ gon-na

Optional Ending

praise You. __   I'm __ gon-na praise You.

THE STORM IS OVER NOW

Words and Music by
R. KELLY

Moderately slow

I tried to force a laugh, but my lips wouldn't lie. My heart was broken,
(Da, da, __ da.)

but I was too sad to even cry. Yet I had to stand my test; I had to take the pain,
(Do you hear me?) (Yeah.) __

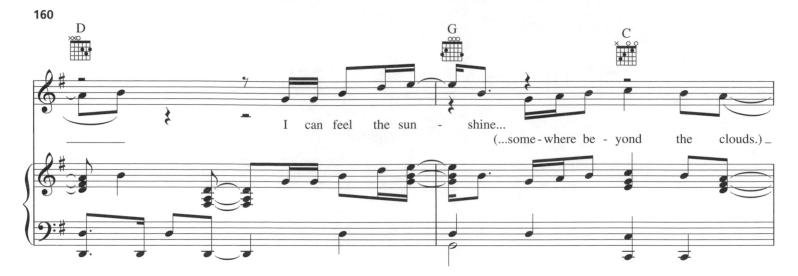

I can feel the sun - shine...
(...some - where be - yond the clouds.) _

It's o - ver now, o - ver now.
(Heav - en is o - ver me.) _

Soprano lead: So come on and set me free. _
(Set me free.) _

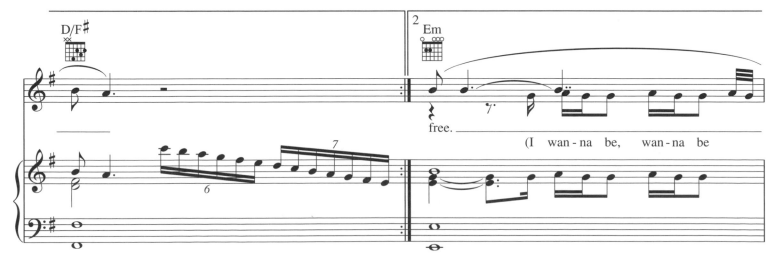

free. _
(I wan - na be, wan - na be

Some - how, my be - gin - ning stepped right in, __
(free.)

__ and faith be - came _ my _ friend. Now I can de - pend on the voic - es of __ the

wind _____ when they say... _____
Tenor lead: I hear them say - ing, *Choir:* I hear them (say - ing,) __

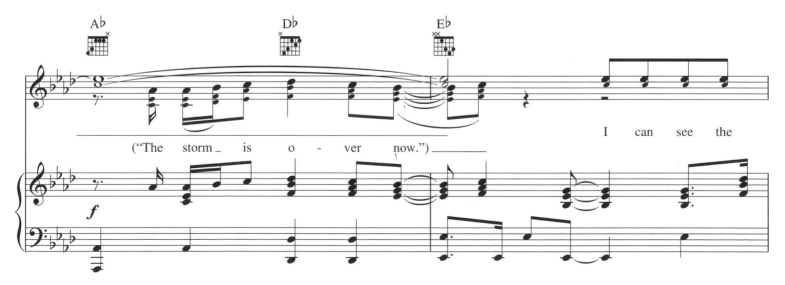

("The storm _ is o - ver now.") _____
I can see the

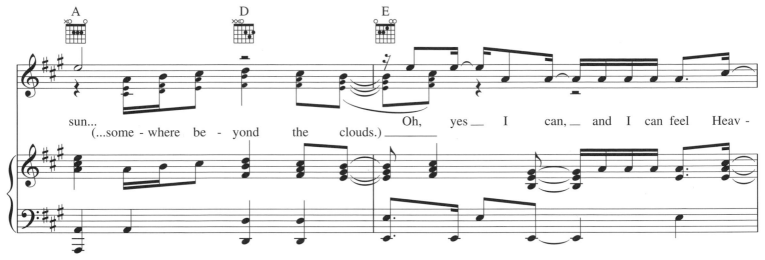

sun...
(...some - where be - yond the clouds.) Oh, yes __ I can, __ and I can feel Heav -

- en. __
(Heav-en is o - ver me.) __ So come on, __ come on, __ and set __ me free. __

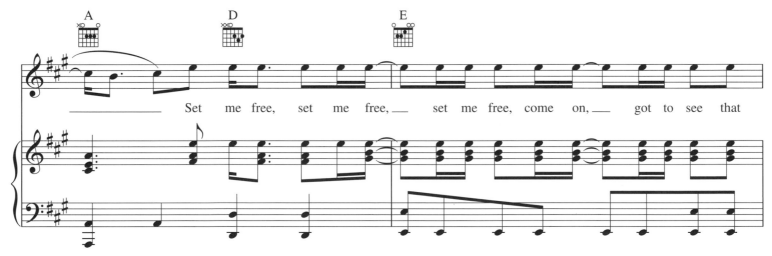

__ Set me free, set me free, __ set me free, come on, __ got to see that

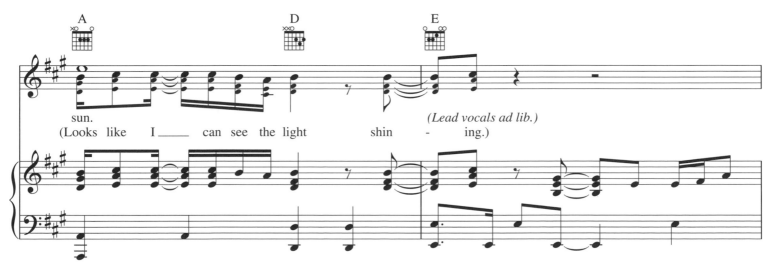

sun.
(Looks like I __ can see the light shin - ing.) *(Lead vocals ad lib.)*

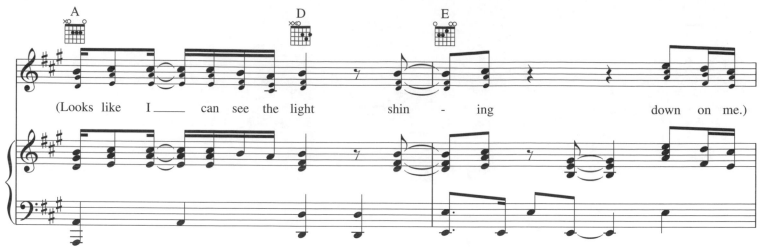

(Looks like I ____ can see the light shin - ing down on me.)

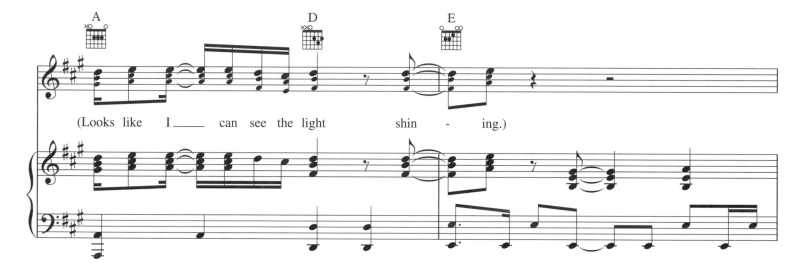

(Looks like I ____ can see the light shin - ing.)

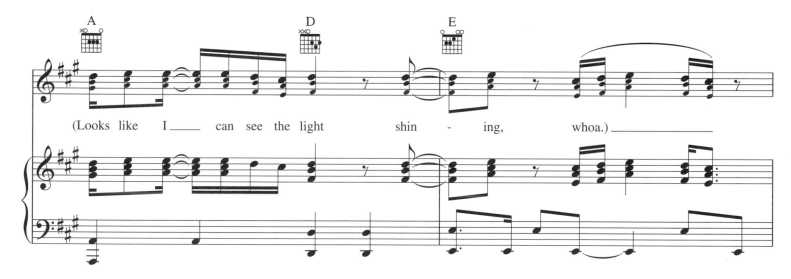

(Looks like I ____ can see the light shin - ing, whoa.) _____

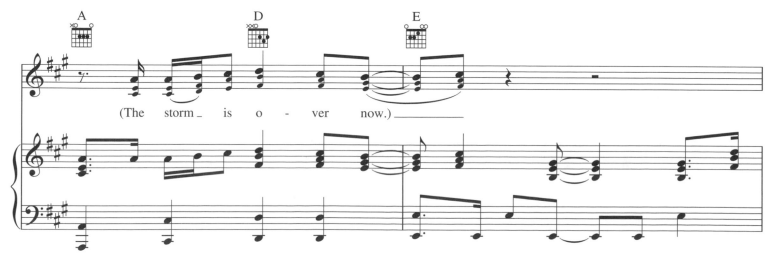

(The storm ___ is o - ver now.) _____

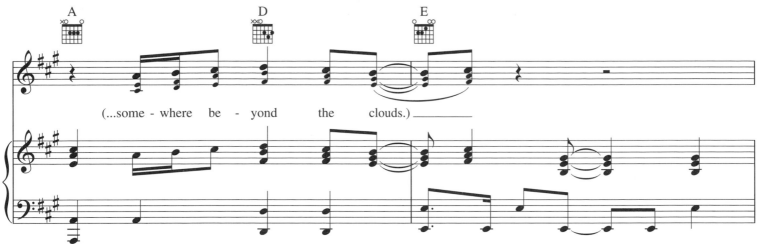

(...some - where be - yond the clouds.) _____

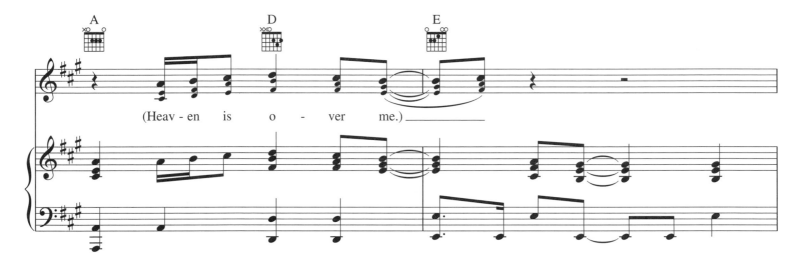

(Heav - en is o - ver me.) _____

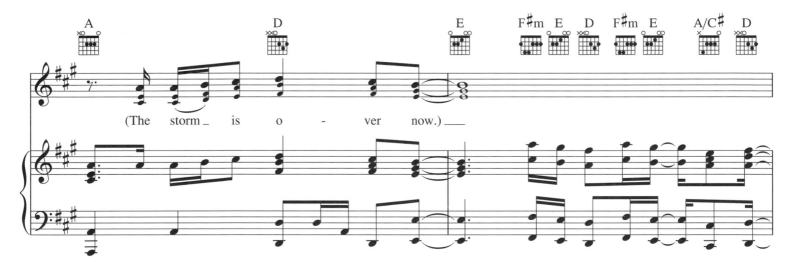

(The storm _ is o - ver now.) ___

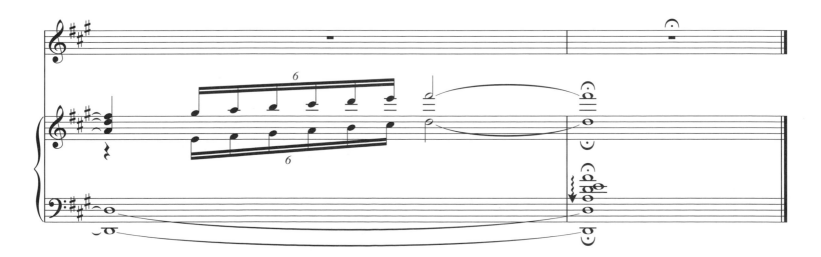

SHAKE YOURSELF LOOSE

Words and Music by VICKIE WINANS
and ANTUN FOSTER

Moderately fast

1st time only (Choir):

Since you been bound up, look-in' for a way to break free,

2nd time only (Lead vocal):

I heard you were feel-in' down, __ that Sa-tan had __ you bound. __

(1., 2.) I want you to know, _____ you're a - bout to break

through.

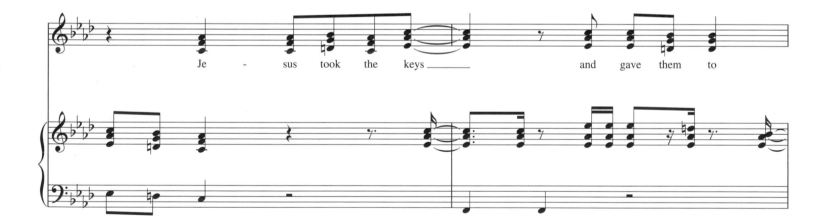

Je - sus took the keys _____ and gave them to

you.   Shake

and do the Da - vid's dance.

1st time only: Don't let the en - e - my

2nd time only: Those chains that bind you ___ should

Bdim

keep you and bind you. Praise ___ your way through. Come on ___

on - ly re - mind you to praise ___ your way through. Come on ___

Ddim   Fm7

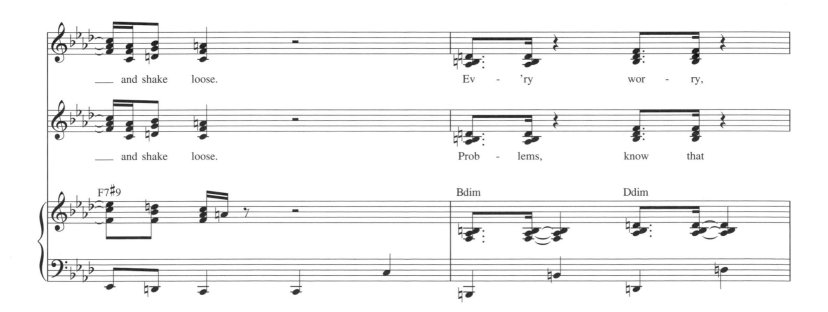

___ and shake loose.   Ev - 'ry wor - ry,

___ and shake loose.   Prob - lems, know that

F7#9   Bdim   Ddim

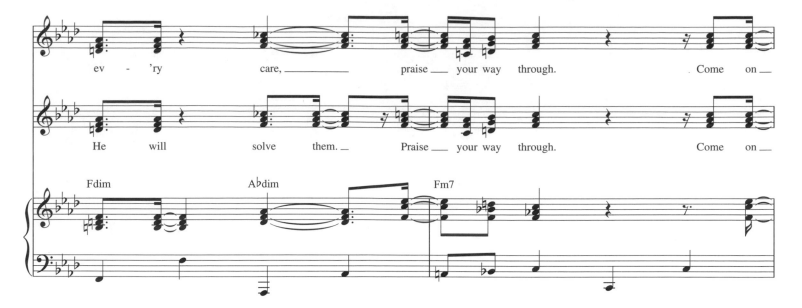

ev - 'ry care, _____ praise _____ your way through. Come on _____

He will solve them. _____ Praise _____ your way through. Come on _____

Fdim   Abdim   Fm7

1

_____ and shake loose.

2

_____ and shake loose.

F7#9   F7#9

(Lead vocal ad lib.)

Shake your - self loose. _____

Lift those hands;
Scream and shout;
Lose your seat,
Shout for joy,

Fm

8vb to end

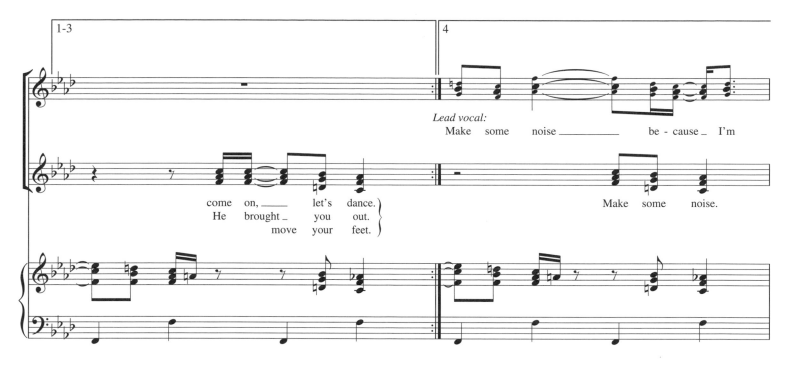

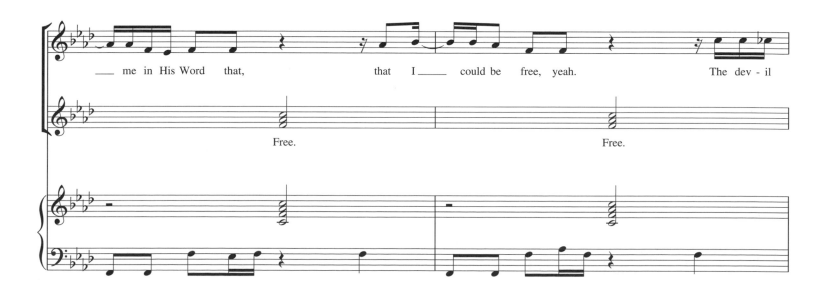

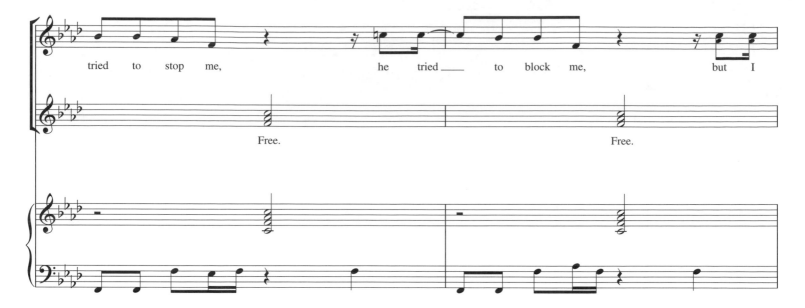

tried to stop me, he tried___ to block me, but I

Free. Free.

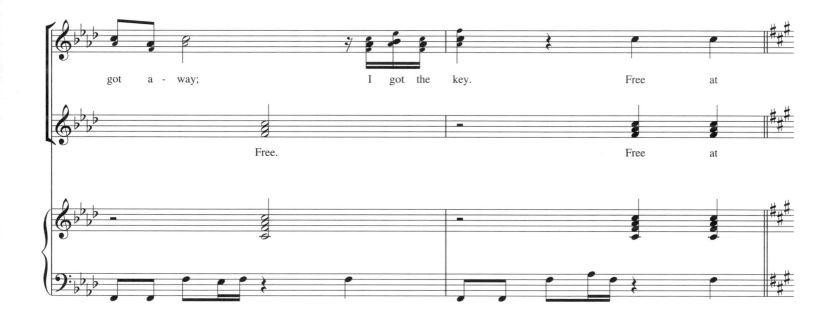

got a - way; I got the key. Free at

Free. Free at

last. Thank___ God Al-might-y I'm... Whom the

last. Free. Free.

Son sets free ___ is free in-deed. ___ He

Free. Free.

loosed the shack-les that was bind-ing me, so get on your feet and sing ___

Free. Free. Free.

___ with me. Those ___ of you out there feel-in' bound, let me tell ___

Free at last.

Gm

you, you can break free, break free. Those ___ of you out there feel - in' bound, let me tell ___

Free.

you, you can break free, break free. Those ___ of you out there feel - in' bound, let me tell ___

Free.

you, you can break free, break free. Those ___ of you out there feel - in' bound, let me tell ___

Free.

you, you can break free, *(Lead vocal ad lib. to end)*

Free at last. Free.

Free. Free.

Play 3 times

Free. Shake your-self loose!

SHOW UP!

Words and Music by
JOHN KEE

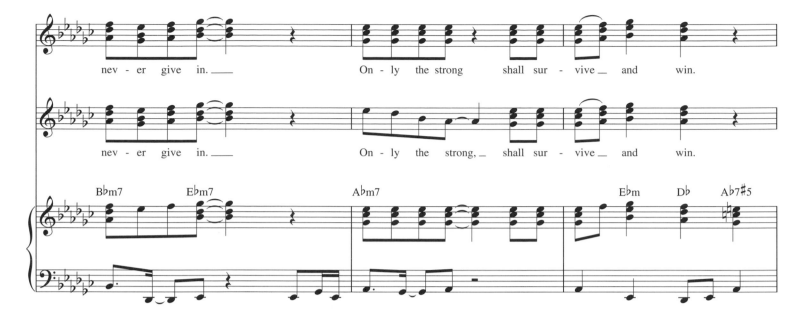

never give in. ___ On - ly the strong shall sur - vive ___ and win.

never give in. ___ On - ly the strong, ___ shall sur - vive ___ and win.

B♭m7   E♭m7   A♭m7   E♭m   D♭   A♭7#5

(1., 2.) Just ask the ques - tion, and the an - swer shall come. Just ex - er - cise your faith, and

D♭m9   G♭13   Am/C   E♭m7   D♭m9

know He's the One. If there is no sign, ___ keep this in mind: ___ He'll show ___

G♭13   E♭7 5(#9)   A♭m7   G♭/D♭   B♭m7   E♭7   A♭m7

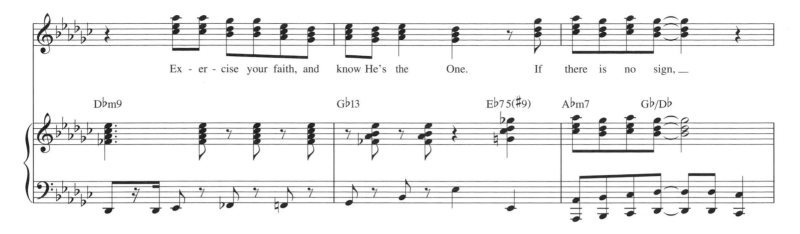

Ex - er - cise your faith, and know He's the One. If there is no sign, __

D.S. al Coda

keep this in mind: __ He'll show __ up on time. __ If there

CODA

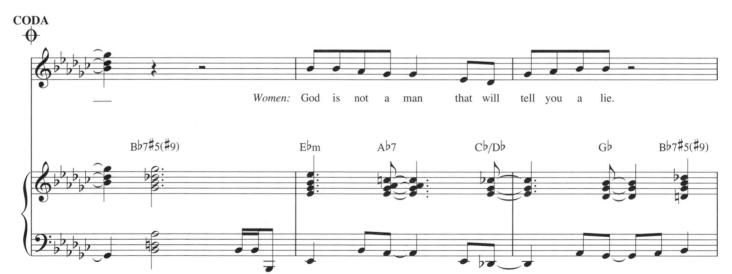

Women: God is not a man that will tell you a lie.

If He tells you so, on Him you can re - ly. God is not a man that will

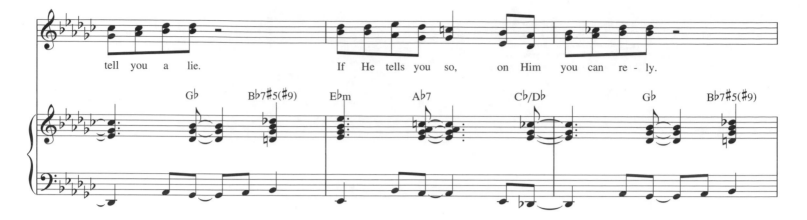

tell you a lie. If He tells you so, on Him you can re - ly.

Gb Bb7#5(#9) Ebm Ab7 Cb/Db Gb Bb7#5(#9)

God is not a man that will tell you a lie. If He tells you so, on Him

Men: God is not a man... tell you a lie. If He tells you so...

Ebm Ab7 Cb/Db Gb Bb7#5(#9) Ebm Ab7 Cb/Db

you can re - ly. *Choir:* If there is no sign, ___ if

you can re - ly.

Gb Abm7 Gb/Db Bbm7 Ebm7

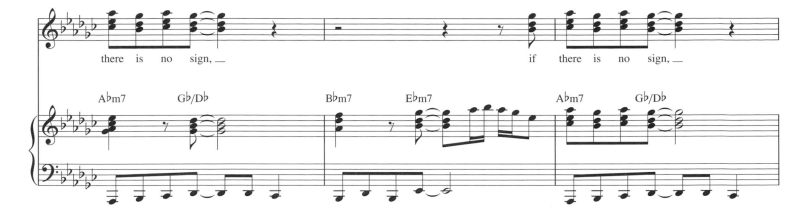

there is no sign, ___ if there is no sign, ___

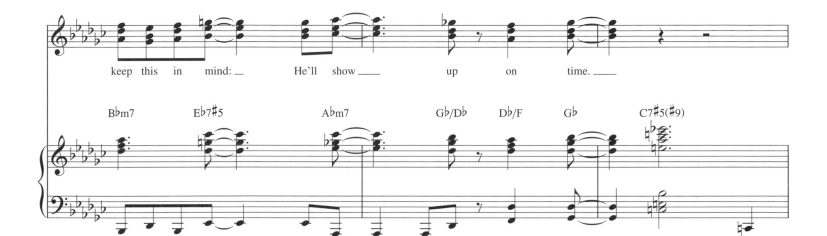

keep this in mind: ___ He'll show ___ up on time. ___

Show up! Show up! Show up!

He'll show up on time. Show up! Show up!

Show up! He'll show up on time. Show up!

Show up! Show up!

Show up! Show up! Show up!

Show up!

Show up! ... Show up!

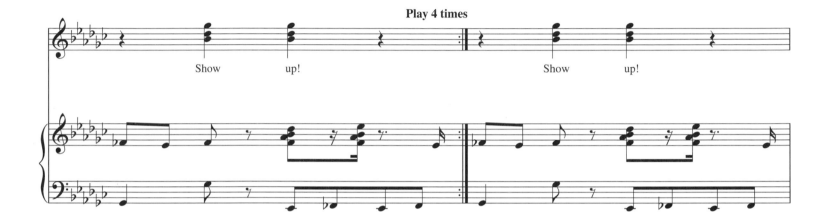

Show up! ... Show up!

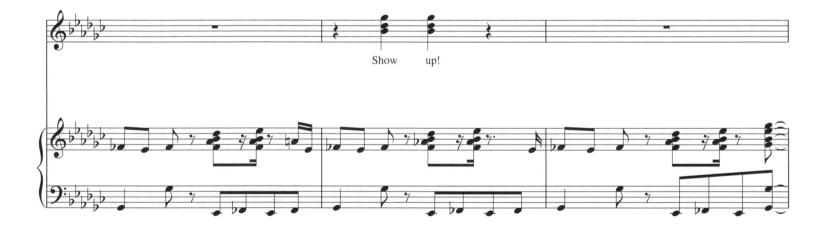

Show up!

Show up!

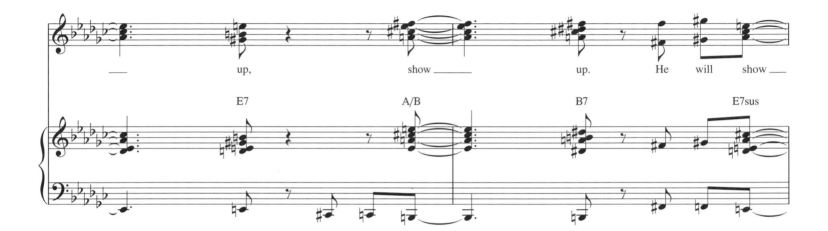

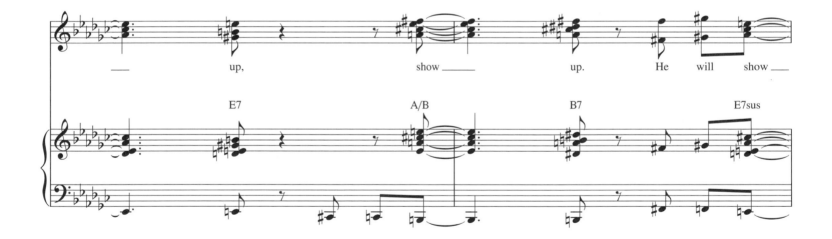

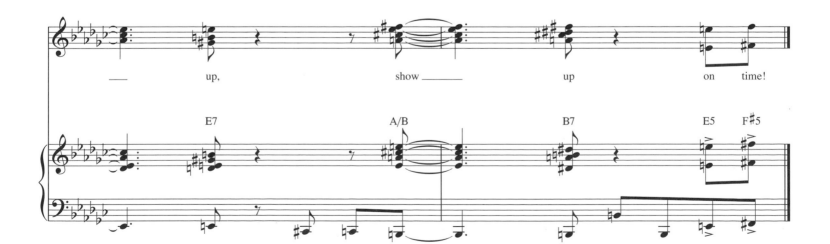

WHY ME

Words and Music by FRED JERKINS III,
LASHAWN DANIELS and KENYATTA JERKINS

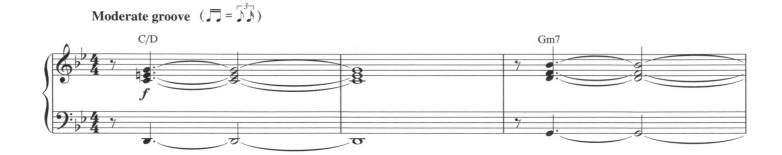

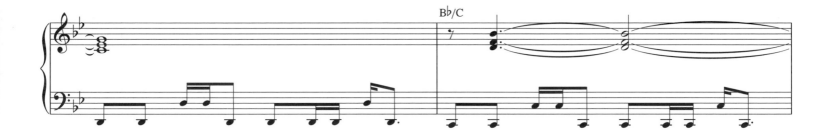

Now why (why) ain't it e-nough that You

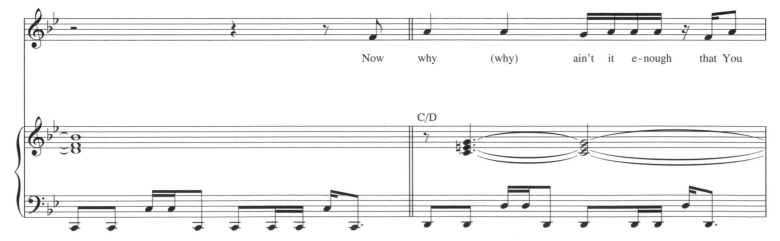

ev - er come to love some-bod - y like You love me,_____ keep some-bod - y like You kept me? _____ (Kept

(Love me.) _____

me.) _____ (Whoa, _____ whoa, why me?) When _ I'm wrong _____ (wrong) and I think You've moved _

_ on (on), You reach out Your hand _ and say, _ "I _ am here. _ I nev-er left _ You, I

brought you here." _ So what makes it hard _ to see? _____ You gave Your own life _ for me, _____

(I love You.)

ev - er come to love some-bod - y like You love me, _____ (Love me.) _____ keep some-bod - y like You kept me? _____ (Kept

Whoa, _____ Lord, why me? And, ooh, I was think - in', _____ how did You me.) _____

ev - er come to love some-bod - y like You love me, _____ (Love me.) _____ keep some-bod - y like You kept me? _____ (Kept

Whoa, _____ Lord, why me? And, ooh, I was think - in'. _____ me.) _____

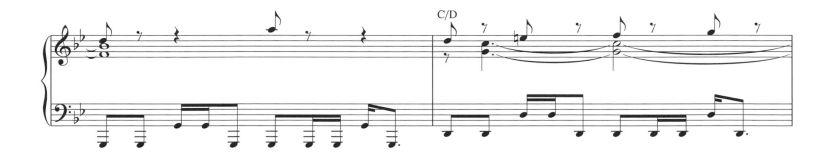

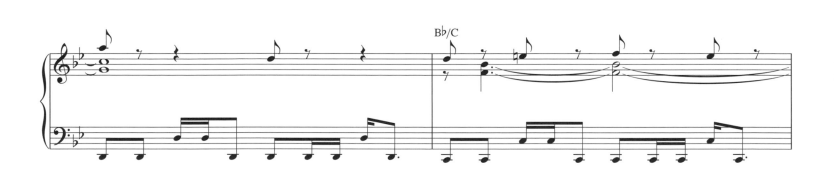

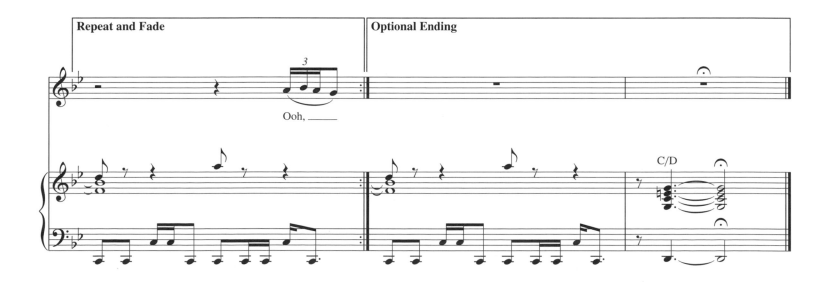

TURN IT AROUND

Words and Music by ISRAEL HOUGHTON
and AARON LINDSEY

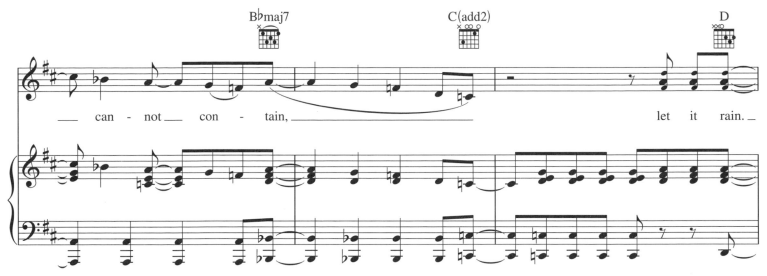

can - not con - tain, _____ let it rain. _____

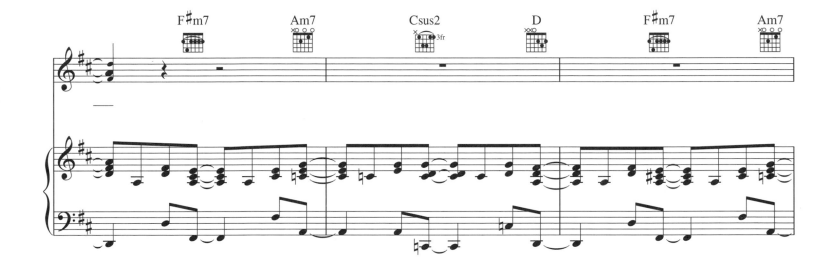

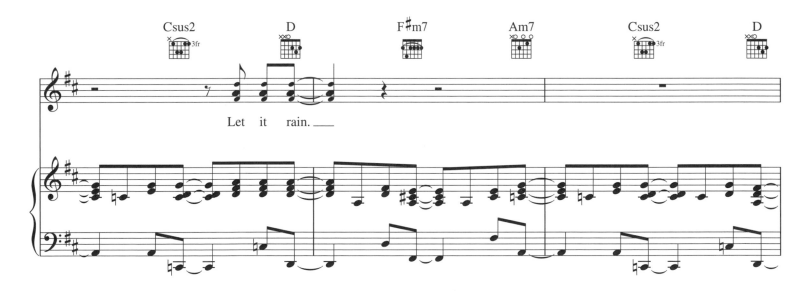

Let it rain. _____

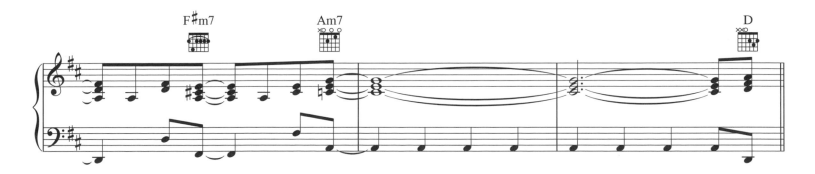

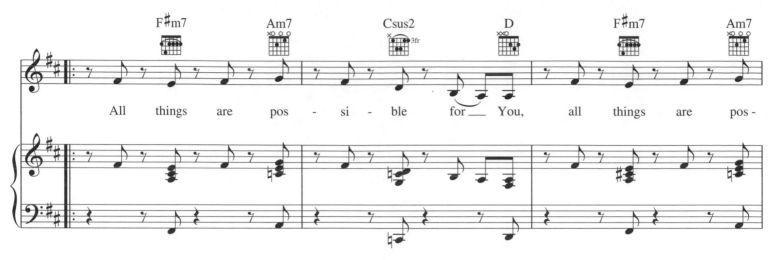

All things are pos - si - ble for ___ You, all things are pos -

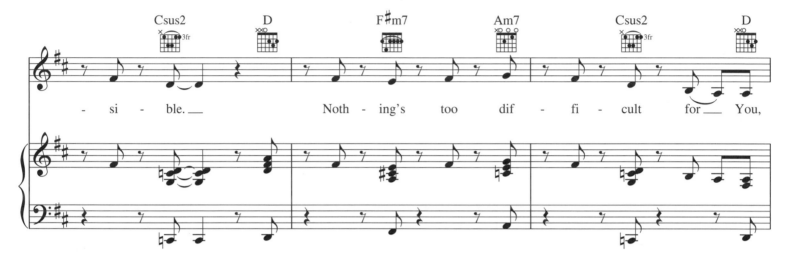

- si - ble. ___ Noth - ing's too dif - fi - cult for ___ You,

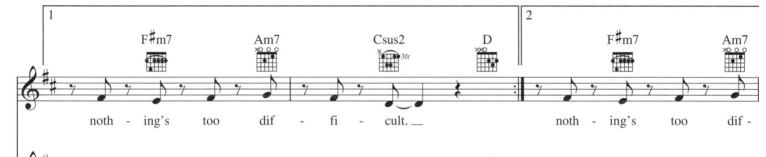

noth - ing's too dif - fi - cult. ___ noth - ing's too dif -

- fi - cult. ___ I'm read - y for change, read - y for rain, read - y for fa -

-vor; I know You're_ a - ble to turn it a - round.__ O - pen the win -

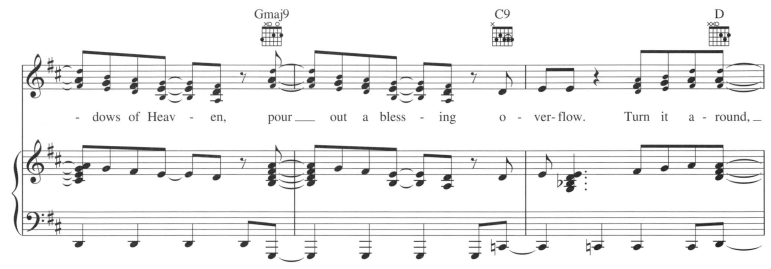

-dows of Heav - en, pour__ out a bless - ing o - ver-flow. Turn it a - round,_

__ o - pen the win - dows of Heav - en, pour__ out a bless - ing we_

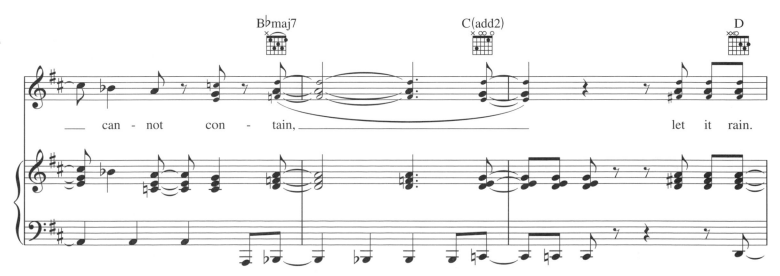

__ can - not con - tain,_____ let it rain.

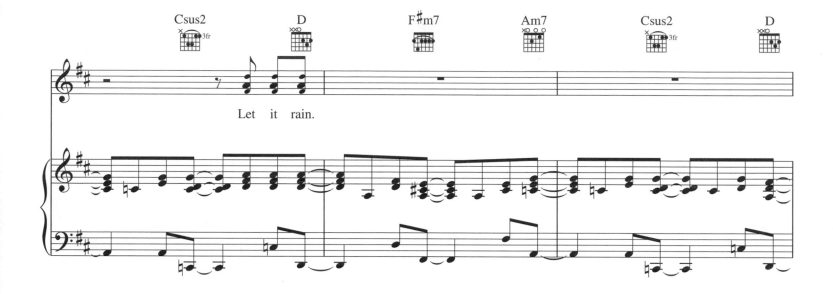

Let it rain.

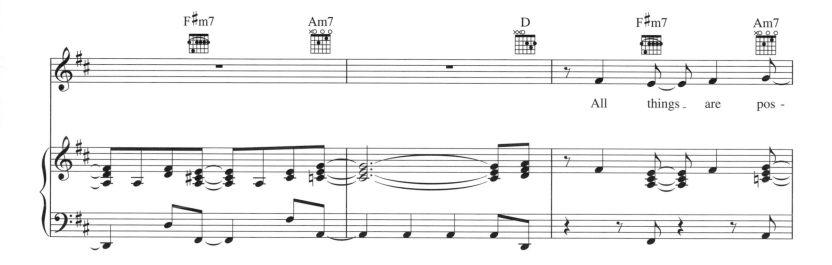

All things _ are pos -

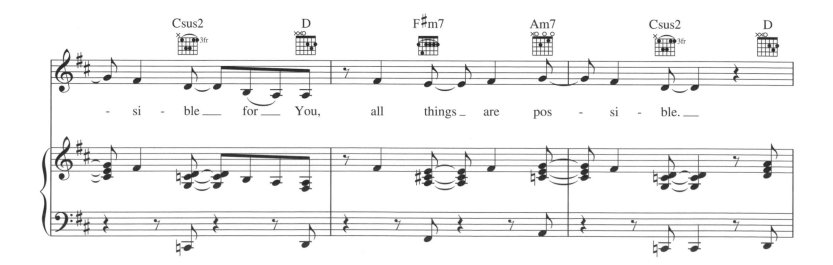

- si - ble _ for _ You, all things _ are pos - si - ble. _

Noth - ing's_ too_ dif - fi - cult_ for_ You, noth - ing's_ too_ dif -

fi - cult. I'm read - y for change, read - y for rain, read - y for fa -

- vor; I know You're_ a - ble_____ to turn it a - round._

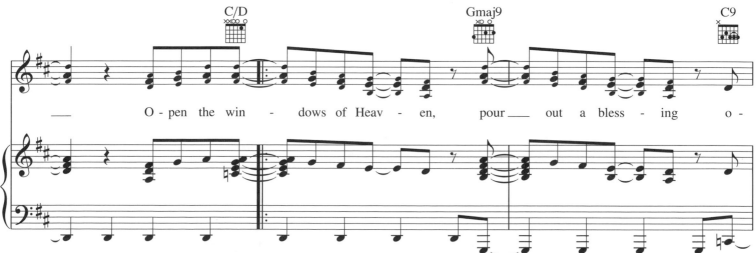

___ O - pen the win - dows of Heav - en, pour___ out a bless - ing o -

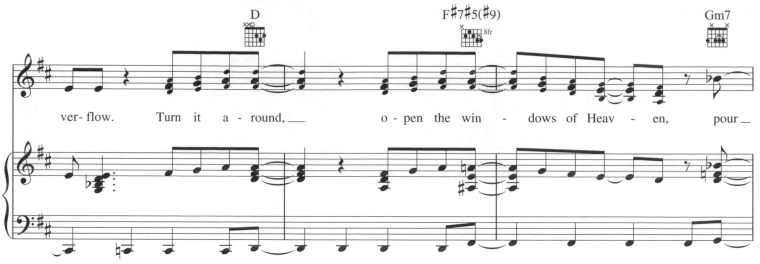

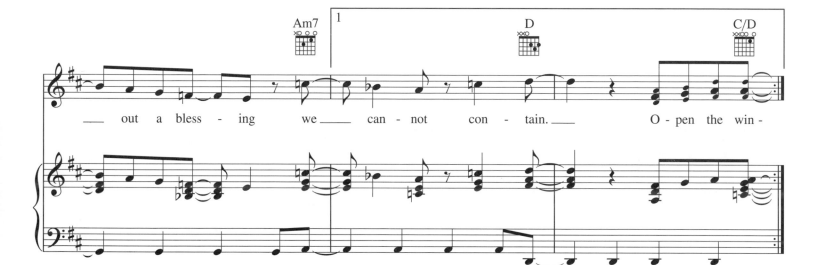

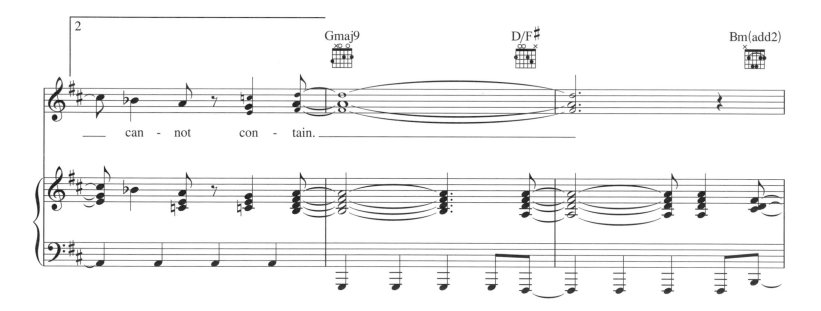

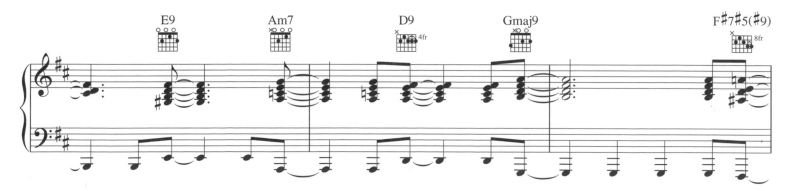

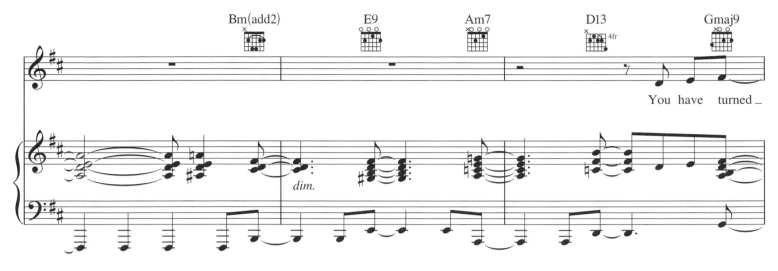

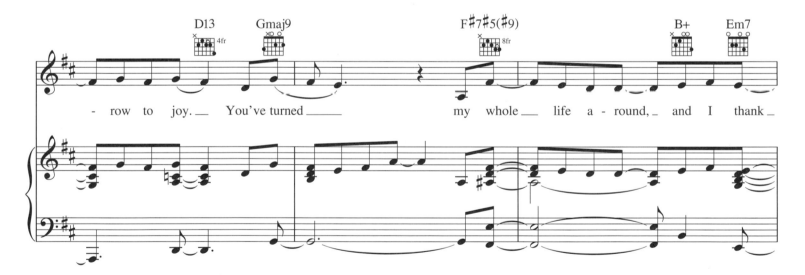

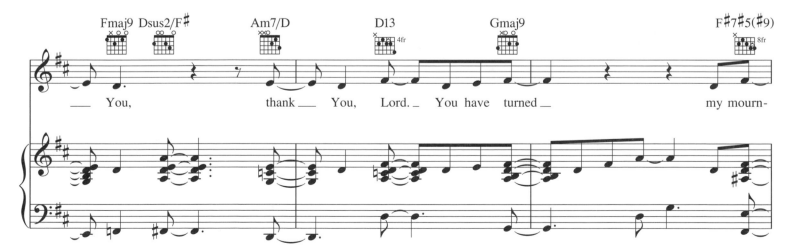

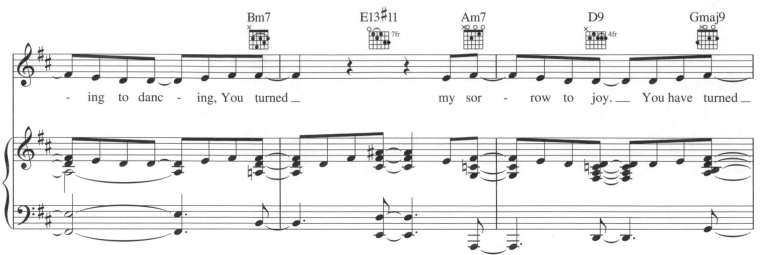

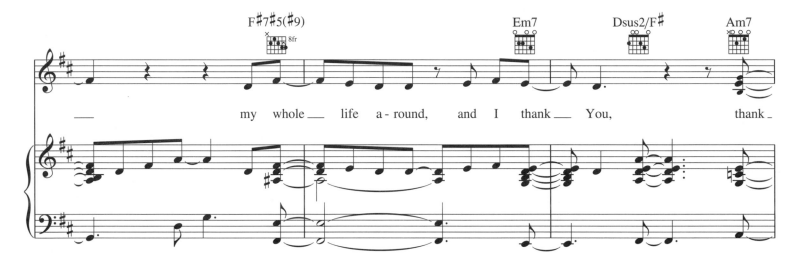

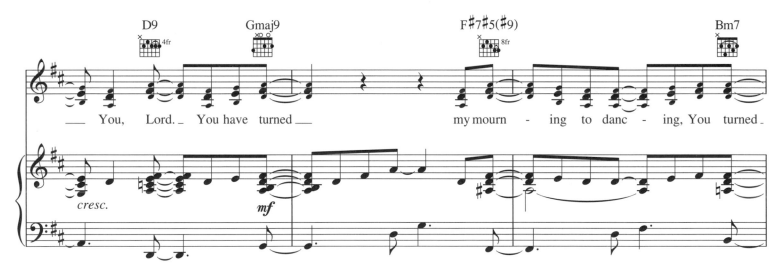

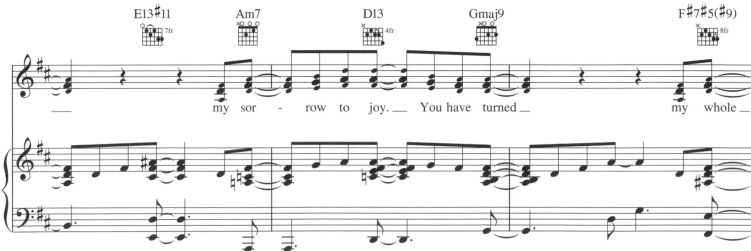

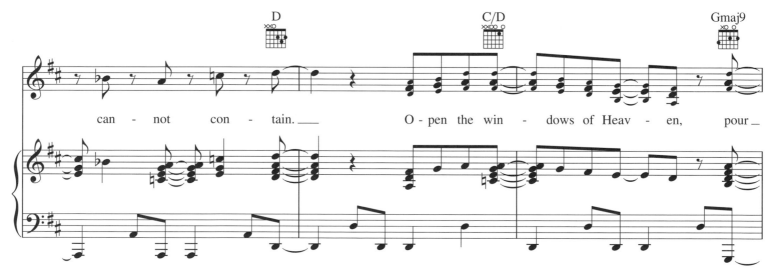

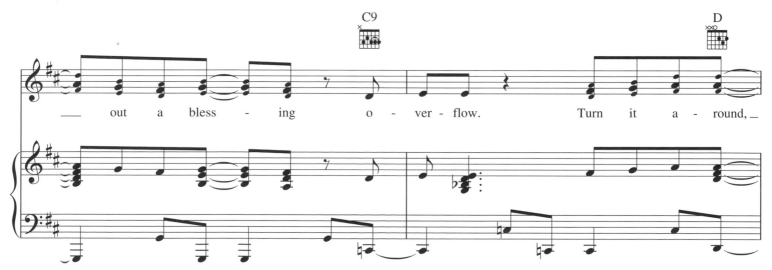